The Big Deal About Alcohol
What Teens Need to Know About Drinking

Marilyn McClellan

Enslow Publishers, Inc.

40 Industrial Road	PO Box 38
Box 398	Aldershot
Berkeley Heights, NJ 07922	Hants GU12 6BP
USA	UK

http://www.enslow.com

Library of Congress Cataloging-in-Publication Data

McClellan, Marilyn.
    The big deal about alcohol : what teens need to know about
drinking / Marilyn McClellan.— 1st ed.
        v. cm. — (Issues in focus)
    Includes bibliographical references and index.
    Contents: Tyler and Lani — The history of alcohol — Alcohol and
the human body — Alcohol and the law — The high cost of alcohol
abuse — The sale of alcohol — Adolescents and alcohol — Current
alcohol issues.
    ISBN-10: 0-7660-2163-7
    1. Alcoholism—United States—Prevention—Juvenile literature.
2. Teenagers—Alcohol use—United States—Juvenile literature.
3. Drinking of alcoholic beverages—United States—Juvenile
literature. [1. Alcohol. 2. Alcoholism] I. Title. II. Issues in focus
(Hillside, N.J.)
    HV5066.M33   2004
    362.292—dc22
                               2003026604
ISBN-13: 978-0-7660-2163-1

Printed in the United States of America

10 9 8 7 6 5 4 3

To Our Readers: We have done our best to make sure all Internet
Addresses in this book were active and appropriate when we went to
press. However, the author and the publisher have no control over and
assume no liability for the material available on those Internet sites or
on other Web sites they may link to. Any comments or suggestions can
be sent by e-mail to comments@enslow.com or to the address on the
back cover.

Illustration Credits: The ARC, p. 41; ArtToday, pp. 14, 22, 73,
86, 91, 110; Campus Health Service, University of Arizona,
p. 97; Corbis Images Royalty-Free, pp. 8, 53; Distilled Spirits
Council of the United States, p. 31; Library of Congress, pp. 25,
69; Donel McClellan, pp. 35, 49, 56, 76, 79, 106.

Cover Illustration: Corel Corporation (background); Corbis
Images Royalty-Free (inset).

Contents

1

Tyler and Lani

Tyler DuHart turned seventeen on Friday, March 26, 1999. That night he and some longtime friends went to a party. They were all high school juniors in Bellingham, Washington. Around ten in the evening, Tyler and his buddies left the party in a black 1995 Chevy Blazer.

The boys were having a great time. They were listening to loud punk rock music and traveling fast. They turned on to a two-lane county road with narrow shoulders and a speed limit of thirty-five miles per hour. The Blazer took a curve at high speed. The driver lost control of the vehicle. It rolled several times down an embankment. The roof hit a large tree stump. The Blazer came to a stop on the passenger side. The top of the vehicle was crushed into the interior. The boys were pinned under the roof. Rescue workers had to remove the roof to get to the boys. They pulled Tyler out of the smashed windshield, strapped him to a backboard, and loaded him into an ambulance. Tyler had been wearing a seatbelt.

Tyler remembers little about the crash. He awakened in the hospital thirty-six hours later wearing a neck brace. He was unable to move his left hand or his right foot. He had a broken neck and bruises on his brain. His speech was slow and his memory faulty. He found out later that his injuries were a millimeter away from paralyzing him for life.[1] Two of the boys were killed instantly in the crash. The driver was critically injured and died two days later. Tyler was the only survivor.

The Response

The school district's crisis response team reported to the high school on Monday. But about three hundred students stayed away from school that day. Groups of friends gathered at homes to console each other. They brought flowers, photos, candles, and other mementos to leave at the crash site. When the students did go back to school, many of them spoke to crisis team members. The team roamed the halls for a week and listened to students talk about their pain.

Few young people voluntarily discussed whether the boys had been drinking. A veil of silence covered that aspect of the accident. The police experienced the same situation. At the site of the crash, and later when talking to friends of the victims, many people indicated that they smelled alcohol on some of the boys' breath. Few reported actually seeing them drink. No one admitted to serving them alcohol. The police report later confirmed that alcohol had been involved.[2]

Kathryn Blair was a friend of the boys. She heard about the crash from a friend who telephoned her. She was stunned. The year following the incident, she wrote in her college entrance essay:

> I know now that I am not invisible, I am not just a bystander in life, but a player like everyone else is. I am just as susceptible to death as any person is and I need to be careful, value and appreciate life's gifts, be nicer to others, and strive toward my goals because you never know what life has in store for you. I honestly feel that I have grown greatly as a person and learned a precious life lesson. It is unfortunate that such a valuable lesson had to be learned from such a horrific tragedy.[3]

Teens Under the Influence

When the boys got into the vehicle, all the odds were against them. It was a weekend. It was nighttime, and other kids were in the car. Two of the boys were unrestrained. For teens, even a very low dose of alcohol can cause impairment. Alcohol can impair a person's ability to divide his or her attention between multiple tasks such as driving and talking to friends in the car or listening to music. It can slow a young

Car accidents can be one tragic result of alcohol misuse.

driver's ability to respond to an emergency. It can distort perception and slow reaction time. It is not uncommon for such terrible tragedies to happen in a blink of an eye.

Although underage drinking is against the law, it is not unusual for teens to drink. According to a report by the Inspector General of the United States Department of Health and Human Services, each year students in junior and senior high schools in America consume 1.1 billion cans of beer.[4] A national survey showed that in one month of 2001, 22 percent of eighth graders used alcohol, along with 39 percent of tenth graders and 50 percent of twelfth graders.[5] The survey indicated that 30 percent of high school seniors were binge or heavy drinkers.[6] (Binge drinking is commonly defined as five or more drinks in a row for men and four or more for women.)

Tyler has not had it easy since the accident. He returned to high school but could not avoid drinking and taking drugs. He did this for more than a year and a half after the crash. Eventually he dropped out of school. He got his high school equivalency certificate in April 2000. That November he checked himself into a treatment center in eastern Washington and tried to deal with the tragedy and the loss in his life. He has been in other automobile accidents since the fatal crash that killed his friends. Each time he has escaped injury.[7]

Lani's Story

When Lani was in the eighth grade, her mother went to a party and disappeared for three days. When she finally came home again, Lani's mother could not remember what she had done with Lani. This was not new behavior. It was how Lani was raised. Her mother was an alcoholic. Lani had taken care of the household since she was a toddler. She prepared her own meals and fed her mom. She cleaned the house and grocery shopped. She even paid the bills. Lani never lived in one house or went to one school longer than a year.

Lani never knew her father. In fact, her mother had many different boyfriends as Lani grew up. Whenever there was a new "dad" that Lani liked, her mom's drinking would ruin the relationship. Her mom called men a "luxury." "She always got a new one when the old one didn't work," according to Lani. Her mother kept a fifth of vodka under her bed. She needed alcohol to keep her going. She called herself a "maintenance drunk." She also used drugs from time to time. As a little girl, Lani remembers calling her mother's dealer to try to buy something to help her mom get out of bed.

Lani never understood why her mother cared more for alcohol than she did for Lani. Why didn't she just stop drinking? Lani was very lucky to have a grandmother to visit. Her grandmother did not drink and took care of Lani from time to time. In fact, her grandmother wanted to get custody of Lani, but her mother would not give her up. Although Lani always knew her mother had affection for her, she felt that her grandmother actually wanted her and would take good care of her.

When Lani's grandmother died, her world began to fall apart. When she was fifteen, her mother said one day, "By the way, I'm going to jail." At this time, Lani had no place to look for guidance. She began her own serious drinking. She really did not like the taste of alcohol. She drank only to get drunk and lose control. By age sixteen, she was drinking heavily and sometimes did not even remember what she had done or where she had been. She reports that one day she simply looked into the mirror. She got scared by what she saw looking back at her. She looked like her mom. Lani stopped drinking.

Today, Lani is married, clean and sober, and training to be a nurse. She tries to be a role model for her three children. She worries that they may have a predisposition to alcohol abuse. She has lived in the same house for seven years. Her mother died two years ago. Lani says, "My mother was intelligent. I always thought she had great potential. The hardest thing I ever did was to let go of my hopes for her. She was just too sick to ever get better." Lani considers herself her grandmother's second chance at raising a healthy, well-functioning child.[8]

Alcohol is a beverage enjoyed by millions of moderate users without devastating effects. It is central to many cultural and social customs such as weddings and parties. From champagne breakfasts to toasts at parties, alcohol is used throughout the world in celebrations. Wine is served at dinner tables across America and in religious rituals that unite congregations in their shared faith. In moderation, alcohol can have a positive effect on health.

Alcohol can also cause devastation. It can be misused and cause fatal accidents and the destruction found in alcoholic families. This book will trace the history of the substance called alcohol, explain alcohol's effects on the body, discuss laws regarding alcohol use, describe alcohol's effect on underage drinkers, and look at some of the issues involved in the production and sale of alcoholic beverages.

2

The History of Alcohol

Humans may have been drinking alcoholic juices since prehistoric times. Birds can be observed flying erratically after feeding upon rotting pyracantha berries. It does not take a leap of imagination to decide that some caveman found that drinking rotting wild fruit juice gave him a feeling of euphoria. The beverage may be as old as human history. Its true beginning remains a mystery.

One legend tells about a prince who stored his grapes in goatskins so he could have them to eat when they were not in season. One of the skins turned bad. He labeled it "Poison." When one of his mistresses got jealous of another woman, she drank the rotting grapes in an attempt to kill herself. Instead of dying, she became intoxicated. She then took a sword and killed her rival. This impressed the prince, who tried the grape drink himself. He enjoyed it so much he began feeding it to his harem to get them drunk.[1]

Yeast is a fungus that is present in many natural habitats. When it comes into contact with grain, fruit, or honey, it begins the chemical process of fermentation. This process converts most of the sugar into carbon dioxide and alcohol. Alcohol is a colorless, odorless, and flammable liquid. By itself, it has a harsh, burning taste. Chemically, it is composed of carbon, hydrogen, and oxygen.

There are many kinds of alcohol. Ethyl alcohol, or ethanol, is the substance found in beverages. During the process of fermentation, the yeast dies when the alcohol concentration reaches about 12–13 percent. The fermentation of grapes and other fruits produces wine. The fermentation of grain produces beer. Fermented honey produces mead.

References to these fermented alcoholic beverages have been found throughout civilized history. They occur as pictographs in cave paintings, in tombs of royalty, and in centuries of ancient writings. Babylonian clay tablets contain beer recipes and illustrations.[2] The intentional brewing of alcohol probably came about with the beginning of agriculture. At that time, grains were harvested and grapes cultivated. This also led to food surpluses and people living closer together in villages or cities. There are references to drinking alcohol in early Egypt and

Mesopotamia. The first mention of alcohol in the Hebrew Bible occurs in the book of Genesis. It is written that Noah drank too much wine made from the vineyards he planted after the Flood.

A wine jar dating around 5000 B.C. was recovered on a dig from a mud-brick Neolithic building in Iran in 1968. It was placed on exhibit at the University of Pennsylvania Museum of Archaeology and Anthropology. Dr. Patrick McGovern, the museum's archeochemist, used modern technology to test the residue found inside of the jar.[3] Amazingly, he was able to detect wine and tree resin thousands of years old.

Alcoholic beverages are mentioned in the records of many ancient civilizations. This drawing shows Egyptians making wine.

In ancient Egypt, beer was an important drink for people of all ages. Early beer production is portrayed on tomb walls. Egyptians sometimes received beer instead of wages for their work.

In an article about ancient Egyptian alcohol, Carolyn Seawright writes that the beer was "nutritious, sweet, without bubbles, and thick (it had to be strained with wooden syphons used as a straw, because it was filled with impurities)."[4] Beer was a staple of the poor. Wine was more expensive and available to the wealthy. The Egyptians may have imported their wine from other countries. They had a word for wine long before grapevines were planted in the Nile valley.[5]

It is not surprising that people of all ages—even children—drank alcoholic beverages. As civilization progressed, people began to cluster in larger numbers in cities and towns. The natural water supply became increasingly contaminated with waste products, making it dangerous to drink. Safe well water and rainwater was not plentiful enough for large populations. Before sewers and water purification systems were invented, alcoholic beverages were safer to drink than most available water.

When alcoholic drinks were diluted with the water supply, the natural acids and antiseptic powers of the alcohol killed many of the pathogens and provided a natural purification. The honey, fruits, grains, and yeast in alcoholic beverages served as a source of nutrition. In fact, the ingredients for making beer, such as grains and yeast, are the same as those used for making bread. Alcohol provided extra calories for people in societies that may have faced continual food shortages. Alcohol was also used for medicinal purposes to clean wounds and relax patients. It provided a sense of euphoria, or well-being, and in some cases relief from pain. Hippocrates cited wine as a remedy for almost all known ailments.[6]

It is believed that the early beverages had a relatively low alcoholic content. Their acids and placement in open containers most likely caused them to resemble vinegar more than wine. Wine today is manufactured and tightly bottled. Sometimes it is fortified with more alcohol. In fermentation alone, the yeasts cannot tolerate high percentages of alcohol. Despite the relatively low strength of early alcoholic beverages, sufficient amounts could cause a person to lose control of his or her behavior and act in inappropriate ways. One of the earliest recorded attempts by a society to control the negative effects of alcohol use dates back to about 1720 B.C. Hammurabi, a king of Babylon, gave tavern-keepers rules about the price of beer and strategies for dealing with drinking disorders. Egyptian papyrus contains prohibitions on excessive drinking and the evils of getting drunk.[7]

Greeks and Romans were noted for their drinking. Plato's *Symposium* speaks of wine within intellectual circles. Many cultures include references to alcohol as part of their religion. Dionysus was the Greek god of wine. Bacchus was the Roman god of wine. For Jews, wine played an important part in ceremonies and celebrations. The Christian Bible talks about Jesus turning water into wine at the wedding in Cana. But there are also biblical warnings against drunkenness, which was frowned upon. Monasteries were well known for their wine making and vineyards. But the Roman Catholic Church had a multitude of laws and regulations against the "sin of intemperance."[8] Other religions also had laws about drinking. Buddha believed in abstaining from intoxicating beverages. Buddhists were urged to follow if they wished to achieve higher states of existence.[9] The prophet Mohammed banned alcohol to those of the Islamic faith, and religious Hindus were expected to abstain.

Around 800 A.D., an Arabian invention called distillation made it possible to make beverages with a highly concentrated form of alcohol. Adding distillation to the fermentation of grapes, grains, molasses, or other sugars and starches produced the first liquors. Distillation boils away alcohol from its sugar bath and re-collects it as virtually pure alcohol.[10] Because pure alcohol is unfit to drink, it is diluted with water to produce liquors or spirits. Other substances called congeners are added to give it a particular flavor or characteristic. Distillation made it possible to produce such liquors as bourbon, brandy, rum, whiskey, and vodka, which have a greater percentage of alcohol than beer or wine. These can have from 40 percent to 70 percent alcohol, although most have less than 50 percent. The term used for the amount of alcohol in a distilled beverage is *proof*. The percentage of alcohol is half of the proof label. That means a label that says 100 proof contains 50 percent alcohol.[11] It took many centuries until the commercial use of distillation was brought to Europe and the western world.

The New World

When the pilgrims arrived on the *Mayflower* in search of religious freedom, they chose to settle near Boston instead of Virginia as they had planned. One of them wrote it was because of their "victuals [food supplies] being spent, especially our Beere."[12] Sanitary conditions on those crowded ships were deplorable. Fresh water was not readily available. The cooler climate of northern Europe had been perfect for the growing of barley used to make beer. It is not surprising that the travelers brought their "beere" from the Old World to drink on their voyage.

Sanitary conditions were not much improved in America. Immigrants brought diseases such as cholera to their adopted country. From the beginning of colonial times, alcohol use was quite common among men and women. It was the colonists' custom to pause for drinks several times a day. Alcohol was usually found on the family dinner table. Even though alcoholic beverages were plentiful and widely used, overuse was not accepted: Drunkenness was a crime throughout the colonies.

The legal use of alcohol by teenagers was quite common from colonial times until the late 1800s. Many adolescents worked in the fields or mines with adults and were treated with similar privileges. Even younger children were permitted to consume alcoholic beverages if their parents approved. Smaller and diluted drinks were most likely served to children. People used the local taverns for relaxation, town meetings, and political discussions.[13] There were laws to prevent drunkenness and tavern disorders. Landlords were not to sell liquor to drunkards. Even free African Americans were not usually allowed in taverns. Laws also controlled the sale of liquor to American Indians. Colonists did not want these "lesser citizens" to get drunk and disorderly. They feared that such behavior might lead to rebellion.

William Penn constructed a brewery in his new colony of Pennsylvania in 1683. Samuel Adams inherited a brewery from his family. One of George Washington's own handwritten recipes for making beer can be seen at the New York Public Library.[14] But the English grains were not well suited to the New World. They were also costly to import. Apple orchards were easier to grow in the New England climate. New Englanders drifted from drinking beer to cider.[15] John Chapman, the famous Johnny Appleseed, was known for planting apple orchards throughout western Pennsylvania through central Ohio, and into Indiana. Domestic apple trees require cross-pollination to produce adequate fruit. The seed-produced apples were not particularly edible. It may be more accurate to say that he was bringing the gift of alcohol to the frontier in the form of seeds to grow apples for fermented, or hard, apple cider.[16]

For thousands of years, alcoholic beverages helped quench people's thirst. Along with an undrinkable water supply, other beverage options were not available. Before the process of commercial distillation came to America in the 1700s, other beverages began making their way to the New World. Tea was invented in the East over five thousand years ago and coffee in the twelfth-century Middle East. However, it was not until the 1600s that both became popular with the Europeans and colonial Americans. In 1611, the first dairy cows from Europe were shipped to America. For centuries, milk had been a staple drink for those wealthy enough to own dairy animals. Cocoa or hot chocolate became available about the same time. However, boiled-water drinks at first had to depend on natural water supplies. The problems with tainted water would not be settled until the end of the nineteenth century, when water purification methods were available. It was then that soft drinks, flavored drinks, and mineral water were introduced.

The safety of manufacturing alcoholic and other beverages relied on the work of French chemist Louis Pasteur in the nineteenth century. Pasteur found a way to scientifically describe the process of fermentation. He was also responsible for developing a process to rid beer and wine of contaminating microorganisms by sterilization. He developed the modern germ theory, which solved the mystery of diseases such as rabies, anthrax, and cholera. This led to the natural applications such as cleanliness, vaccination, and pasteurization. Pasteur taught the world how to manipulate the germs and viruses that cause disease. This, in turn, led to safer food and water.

Alcohol was responsible for the first test of centralized power in the new nation. In 1791 the federal government imposed an excise tax on the distillation of whiskey. The tax angered the frontier farmers who were small producers of whiskey. It caused a particularly violent reaction in western

Pennsylvania, where farmers staged a series of attacks on government agents. The violence increased until President George Washington issued a proclamation that called out the militia to suppress the insurrection, known as the Whiskey Rebellion. The national government had asserted its right to enforce order among the states.

Temperance

By 1792, there were twenty-five hundred registered commercial distilleries in the United States. That year, the consumption of alcoholic beverages by the average American over fifteen years old was estimated at about thirty-four gallons of beer and cider, along with almost five gallons of distilled liquors and less than one gallon of wine. The amount added up to nearly six gallons of pure alcohol per person each year.[17] At this time the country was changing from a nation of family farms and shops. Men now went to work in factories while women stayed home. Drunkenness became an increasing problem. Absenteeism and poor performance seriously interfered with factory production. The free and easy attitude toward alcohol was becoming a concern. Mounting social problems affected the American home. Drinking appeared to be an activity conducted in public places frequented by men and immoral women. Violence in saloons was a serious problem. Those who drank excessively were called drunks. Women were unable by law to divorce such husbands. Women were also unable to earn a wage outside the home. Since there was little help for families, the wife of a "drunkard" faced brutality, poverty, and abandonment.[18]

Although women were often portrayed as abstainers and virtuous in their fight against alcohol, evidence against these ideas is found in such artifacts as etiquette manuals, cookbooks, and glassware. It points to the fact that alcohol was present in many respectable homes. This contradicts the idea that only unrespectable women drank alcohol.

A movement toward temperance, or moderation, began because coalitions of women, pastors, and civic leaders believed that liquor was a threat to society. They argued that liquor destroyed lives, ravaged

The legal use of alcohol by teenagers and even children was accepted in America through the nineteenth century, as shown in this engraving.

families, eroded morality, and contributed to crime.[19] People were asked to drink alcohol moderately or to refrain from drinking alcohol altogether and choose a nonalcoholic alternative.

The opposition to alcohol became a political issue. The war against drinking was a national conflict between those who believed in the right to drink (the "wets") and those who promoted moderate or no drinking (the "drys"). Women's groups preached temperance. They marched from town to town in protest against the evils of alcohol. Women suffragists joined in the fight. Saloons that were considered male drinking places and hotbeds of prostitution also served as polling places on election day. One of the most visible members of the Prohibition movement was Carry Nation. She went around smashing saloons with her hatchet in her home state of Kansas and other states across the country in the late 1890s. Suffragists knew that male drinking and male politics were intertwined. A suffragist was quoted as saying, "You will not have ballot-boxes in saloons when your wives and daughters have votes."[20]

Prohibition and the Eighteenth Amendment

The temperance movement soon blossomed into a full-fledged campaign. Coalitions of citizens such as the Women's Christian Temperance Union and the Anti-Saloon League formed political groups. In 1851 the first Prohibition law was passed in Maine. It removed licenses from establishments in that state that sold liquor. Many states followed with similar laws. By 1917, twenty-seven states were "dry," as well as many cities and counties in the remaining states. During that same year, the American Medical Association took a new stand. They declared their belief that alcohol was detrimental to health, that it had no therapeutic use and no scientific value.[21]

In 1919, the United States government passed two important Prohibition laws. It ratified the Eighteenth Amendment to the U.S. Constitution, which made the "manufacture, sale or transport" of intoxicating liquors illegal. It became illegal to import and export alcoholic beverages. Congress also passed the Volstead Act, banning the use of grain for brewing and distilling. It defined the illegal beverage as any product having 0.5 percent alcohol content or higher. Interestingly, the Prohibition laws allowed medicinal and religious use of alcoholic beverages through prescription. It also allowed the limited manufacture and distribution when those supplies were low.

Prohibition was a sad but colorful part of U.S. history. The public demand for alcoholic beverages proved stronger than the forces of law. Prohibition drove drinking underground and created new opportunities for bootleggers, dishonest government officials, and corrupt police officers. These groups all profited from the illegal alcohol trade. Organized crime flourished. The loss of income to the government from the alcohol industry was huge.

It was difficult for the states to enforce Prohibition. Between 1921 and 1923, about seven thousand persons were arrested for breaking Prohibition laws in New York. However, only twenty-seven were convicted.[22] People who were determined to drink, drank. The state of New York went from having fifteen thousand legal bars to having thirty-two thousand illegal speakeasies. These were undercover drinking spots where customers whispered passwords in order to be admitted.[23]

Repeal of the Eighteenth Amendment

The public soon tired of the lawlessness that Prohibition had unleashed. In 1930 the American Bar Association adopted a resolution calling for the repeal of Prohibition. In 1933, there was enough support to pass the Twenty-first Amendment to the Constitution. This overturned the Eighteenth Amendment. However, many states chose to remain dry. It would be thirty years until all states allowed alcohol sales again.

There is little doubt that Prohibition was a mistake with terrible consequences. One startling fact was that the

Bootleg, or illegal, alcohol got its name from this ingenious method of hiding liquor bottles.

number of women and college-age young people who began drinking increased during the period. The country had lost control over crime and the illegal production and consumption of alcohol. People died from unregulated bootlegged liquor. As a movement that was intended to reduce crime and solve social problems, it was a failure.

However, there are some who note that a comparison of alcohol sales before and after Prohibition shows a general decrease in drinking in America. The per capita alcohol consumption dipped to about one third of the previous level. Health statistics show that the incidence of treated alcoholism was rarer than before Prohibition. The incidence of many alcohol-related diseases also diminished. The death rate due to drinking declined.[24] This is a controversial subject, however; many people claim that these statistics had shown a downward trend before Prohibition even began. The argument shows that Prohibition was an extremely controversial subject in American history.

As the twentieth century progressed, American drinking habits changed. There was an increase in drinking during the economic boom following World War II. During Prohibition, flavorings had been added to mask the taste of inferior liquor. These sweeter drinks, called cocktails, were now the rage. Wine and beer became more popular in the 1970s. Beer that was once sold in saloons by the glass was now bottled and placed on supermarket shelves for transport and consumption elsewhere.[25] Wine and fruit juice were bottled as wine coolers in the 1980s. It took over thirty years for the per capita drinking rate as measured by the legal sale of alcohol to rise until it matched the decade before Prohibition. The addition of sweetened alcoholic drinks and lower calorie wines and beers increased the appeal of drinking alcohol to a variety of drinkers, including the young and the calorie conscious.

During the last quarter of the twentieth century, government agencies and national organizations such as Mothers Against Drunk Drivers (MADD, now known as Mothers Against Drunk Driving) and Students Against Driving Drunk (SADD, now known as Students Against Destructive Decisions), have pushed for legislation against the nation's drunk drivers and alcohol abuse by the young. Some of the cultural perceptions about drinking started to change. Consumption rates in the country declined from 1981 until 1997.[26] The 1989 Gallup Poll reported that 44 percent of Americans were not drinking at all.[27] The hilarious drunk who had been pictured in the media and popular films as the life of the party began to be viewed as an unwelcome pest. Companies frowned on reimbursing employees who took long three-martini lunches with their clients. College campuses began education programs for their students who consumed alcohol. Dry dorms appeared on some campuses. Fraternities and sororities were ordered by their sponsors to give up hazing practices that involved excessive use of alcohol.

About 10 percent of drinkers account for half the alcohol consumed in the United States. Women continue to drink less than men, but the gender gap is closing. Illegal teen drinking is a societal problem.

Younger adults drink more than older adults. Many states have added alcohol education programs in their schools. The federal government and a variety of interest groups have worked hard to increase awareness about the costs of alcohol abuse in the society. Many new laws have been passed to curtail underage and irresponsible drinking. Americans are still drinking—and some are drinking excessively. But it appears that the nation wishes to regulate its own habits, educate persons into sobriety, and teach citizens that if they choose to drink, they need to do so responsibly.

3

Alcohol and the Human Body

Standards and customs change over time. Alcoholic beverages evolved from being a commonly used everyday mealtime accompaniment and a medicinal aid into a serious potential health threat. It is a substance so controversial that its legal use caused a major political upheaval in United States history. What is this liquid that has caused so much controversy over the centuries?

The Body Reacts

When a person drinks, about 20 percent of the alcohol is quickly absorbed into the stomach and bloodstream. The rest goes into the small intestine. The alcohol then dissolves in the blood and gets carried throughout the body.

The effects of alcohol are felt when the circulating blood reaches the brain. Alcohol enters all but the fatty tissues to exert its effects. Once alcohol enters the bloodstream, it leaves the body through the kidneys, the lungs, and the liver. The kidneys eliminate 5 percent through urine. The lungs exhale 5 percent. This can be detected by a Breathalyzer. The liver breaks down the remaining alcohol into acetic acid.

A person can drink alcohol more quickly than the body can get rid of it. The higher the concentration of alcohol in a beverage, the faster it is absorbed into the bloodstream. The absorption also speeds up when alcohol is mixed with carbonated beverages. It makes a difference how recently the drinker has eaten. The absorption of alcohol into the small intestine is slower on a full stomach.[1]

The level of alcohol in a person's body is known as the blood alcohol content or concentration (BAC)—also called the blood alcohol level (BAL). The BAC is defined as the ratio of alcohol to blood in the bloodstream. The measurement is expressed in milligrams of alcohol per 1,000 milliliters of blood and given as a percentage. A person with a 0.10 percent BAC has one part alcohol per 1,000 parts blood in the body. A 0.08 percent BAC has a concentration of alcohol in the bloodstream equal to 0.8 parts alcohol for every 1,000 parts of blood. Or, one could say that for every 1,000 milliliters of blood, the body contains eight tenths of a milliliter of alcohol. The

BAC can be measured by a blood, urine, or breath test. It is also possible to estimate the BAC by calculating a person's body weight, sex, and the amount of alcohol he or she has consumed over a specific amount of time.

The blood alcohol concentration in a person's body depends upon a variety of factors. The amount of alcohol varies from drink to drink. For instance, a twelve-ounce beer, a five-ounce glass of wine, and a one and a half-ounce serving of 80-proof liquor each contain about one half ounce of alcohol; each will increase an average person's BAC by 0.02 percent. The BAC is affected by the alcohol content

12 oz   1 1/2 oz   5 oz

Standard servings of beer, distilled spirits, and wine each contain the same amount of alcohol.

of the individual drinks, the number of drinks consumed, and how fast they are taken into the body. If alcohol is taken in faster than the body can process it, the BAC automatically rises.

The amount of time that alcohol stays in the body varies from person to person. It does not depend only on the amount of alcohol that was drunk, but also on the drinker's weight, the amount of food in the stomach, the speed at which that particular person processes alcohol, and how many months or years he or she has been drinking. A general rule of thumb is this: Under normal circumstances, it takes at least one hour for a half ounce of alcohol to leave a fully grown man's body. If he drinks more than this, he is putting alcohol into his system faster than it can be removed.

There is no way to shorten the time it takes for the alcohol to leave the body. There are some myths about getting rid of the alcohol by vomiting, drinking strong coffee, or taking a cold shower. But alcohol is absorbed so quickly that these do not work. Vomiting may actually be dangerous. A person may be more prone to choking on vomit because drinking disrupts motor behavior.[2]

Gender and Size

Alcohol affects women differently from men. A woman will get more intoxicated than a man even if all other factors are the same. A difference of hormones, fluids, or enzyme levels may be part of the reason. Women have more fatty tissue. Alcohol enters a woman's bloodstream faster.

In addition, body weight makes a difference. Two people of different weights will have different blood alcohol contents even if they drink the same amount over the same period of time. Since BAC represents the ratio of alcohol to the fluids in a person's body, someone who weighs 200 pounds and drinks one beer will have a lower concentration than one who weighs 100 pounds and drinks one beer. The bigger a person is, the more the alcohol will be diluted.

BAC and Intoxication

Blood alcohol concentration is used to assess a person's degree of intoxication. As the BAC rises, a person experiences a variety of effects from the alcohol in his or her system. At 0.02 percent BAC—or just one drink—the average adult may feel relaxed and experience slowed reaction time. The relaxation comes from the depression of the central nervous system. Even at this low level, some studies have shown that there is evidence of impairment in the ability to focus attention. At 0.04 percent BAC, a person might begin to make mistakes without recognizing them. Between 0.05 percent and 0.06 percent, a drinker can feel euphoria or giddiness. These feelings are often pleasant as a person feels relaxed and less inhibited. They are the reasons many people drink. But they come at a price. Alcohol decreases the brain's ability to process information. So, while people are feeling happy, their judgment and their fine motor skills deteriorate. They may say the first thought that comes to their mind and regret it later. Each successive drink becomes more of a liability. At 0.08 percent, coordination is decreased. This is the legal adult driving limit in most states. A person might become sleepy, with blurry vision and uncoordinated movements. Decision making is impaired. At 0.10 percent, there is a marked loss of coordination and judgment. Beyond these levels, a person is at risk for blacking out and losing consciousness. Death becomes a possibility. A lethal blood alcohol level is generally around 0.40 percent to 0.45 percent.[3] It is important to remember that alcohol affects different people in a variety of ways; a person with no tolerance and little experience with alcohol will feel the effects at a much lower level BAC than someone with high tolerance and long experience drinking.

The word "intoxication" comes from the word "toxic," meaning poisonous. Alcohol is essentially poisonous to the body in large doses. Because alcohol depresses the central nervous system, drinking too much at one time can cause death. When someone who is addicted to alcohol is trying to get rid of his dependence, he is being "detoxified."[4]

Alcohol dilates or enlarges the blood vessels. It causes a rush of blood to the skin that gives the appearance of warmth. It is also a diuretic, which increases urination. Heavy drinking causes the blood sugar level to fall rapidly.[5] People who drink too much may wake up sick the next morning. Headache, nausea, and vomiting are symptoms of a hangover. There is no precise scientific definition for a hangover. Excessive alcohol use is hard on the body. There are substances called congeners that help flavor drinks

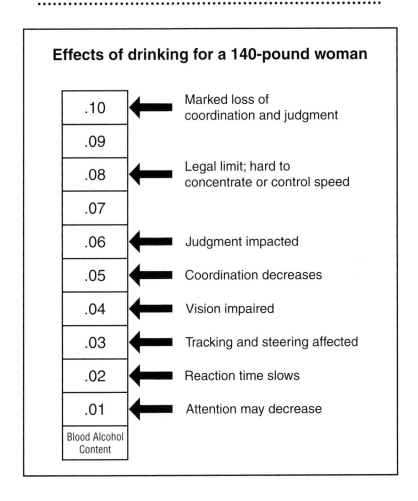

Effects of drinking for a 140-pound woman

BAC	Effect
.10	Marked loss of coordination and judgment
.09	
.08	Legal limit; hard to concentrate or control speed
.07	
.06	Judgment impacted
.05	Coordination decreases
.04	Vision impaired
.03	Tracking and steering affected
.02	Reaction time slows
.01	Attention may decrease

Blood Alcohol Content

that may be part of the cause. Other factors may include dehydration and the physical condition of the drinker. There are no known cures for a hangover. Unfortunately, hangovers have an effect long after the alcohol has left the body. Besides the flu-like symptoms, hangovers cause people to miss work and other productive activities in their normal daily life.

An ounce of alcohol contains the amount of

calories equivalent to those in a baked potato or a glass of milk. It may contain trace levels of vitamins and minerals. However, it is not a good source of nutrition. It is dangerous to replace the calories obtained from healthy foods with those from alcohol. Alcohol can interfere with the complete digestion of food. It robs the body of essential substances. People who abuse alcohol develop malnutrition, regardless of what or how much they eat.[6]

Tolerance

Some people develop a tolerance to alcohol. Over time it may take more and more alcohol to produce the same feelings of euphoria once felt with a few drinks. The body becomes more efficient at eliminating the higher levels of alcohol in the blood. This sets up a vicious cycle of increased drinking just to get the same effects that used to come with fewer drinks. Continued drinking at this level may lead to increased health risks and possible alcohol dependence. People who have built up tolerance are said to be able to "hold their liquor" better than others. However, this is not an advantage. People who do not have tolerance have a built-in warning system of dizziness or nausea to let them know when they drink too much. This prevents them from doing serious damage to their body. Tolerant people drink without recognizing cues that would alert them to stop.

Tolerance develops as a result of physical changes to the brain, the liver, or other organs of the body. The drinker's body adapts to the increasing amount of alcohol taken into the system. In this situation, drinkers may become irritable when not drinking. They may act as if they had less to drink even when their BAC is very high. This is especially dangerous if they get behind a wheel of a vehicle. They do not believe they are intoxicated. It may be possible to reduce tolerance and the health risks that accompany it by cutting down on drinking or stopping it altogether.[7]

Alcohol Dependence

It does not matter how the alcohol is packaged. Beer, wine, and whiskey can all cause dependence or addiction. An alcohol-dependent person—an alcoholic—does not necessarily drink every day. Sometimes a person will have a dependency and drink only on weekends. Dependency has more to do with having an obsessive need and craving for alcoholic beverages even though they cause problems in a drinker's life. Alcoholics are preoccupied with drinking. They have developed tolerance. They experience withdrawal symptoms when they attempt to stop drinking. Although a significant number of persons develop drinking problems that affect their ability to handle normal activities, not all are at risk for addiction.

No one knows why some people become dependent on alcohol and others do not. There are a variety of theories. The development of alcohol dependence seems to be influenced by genetic disposition, family history, environment, and the interaction between the various factors. There are clear indications that there is a genetic disposition to alcoholism. Researchers are still trying to isolate the exact genes. They do know that particular enzymes are involved in the way alcohol is metabolized. Alcohol also interferes with the synapses of the neurotransmitters that carry messages in the brain. This affects the brain's communication system. Prolonged exposure to alcohol may actually change the neurons in susceptible people.[8] As scientists work with genetics and the human genome, they hope to uncover many of these mysteries. Researchers would like to find the key to help people regulate their drinking before it becomes destructive to them.

Anyone who drinks constantly and excessively over time will suffer physical deterioration from the alcohol. Excessive drinkers put themselves at risk for many diseases. Chronic liver disease (cirrhosis), digestive tract diseases such as ulcers, and cancers of the throat, esophagus, and liver are possible health risks. Some of these appear to be directly caused by the effect of alcohol use on the organ. Others may result from a depressed immune system. This is a consequence of inadequate nutrition and extreme alcohol use over time. As scientists uncover ways to scan the brain, they are finding that excessive alcohol use over time also causes damage to cells. Because the body is a marvelous machine with extraordinary healing properties, sometimes organs are able to regenerate if drinking is stopped in time. Many conditions, such as cirrhosis, are irreversible. However, someone who stops drinking might be able to halt the progression of the disease.

Alcoholics often suffer from a variety of psychological problems such as high anxiety and depression.

They have difficulty keeping healthy relationships. Frequently they lie and are secretive about their alcohol use. They often have legal problems.

Alcoholics spend a tremendous amount of energy pretending that they have everything under control. They believe that they can stop drinking at any time they wish. Alcoholics will deny they have a drinking problem even in the face of clear evidence presented to them. This is one reason alcoholics often refuse to get help when they need it. It is called "being in denial."

Blackouts and Withdrawal

Blackouts are a common symptom of an alcohol-dependent person. These are periods of temporary amnesia that can last from a few minutes to several days. During these episodes, drinkers may appear to be aware of their surroundings. However, they are later unable to recall what happened. Although it is possible for a social drinker to experience a blackout, this is normally one of the red flags to indicate that a person might be dependent on alcohol. In a recent study, over seven hundred students at Duke University were surveyed. Nearly three quarters of them said they had drunk alcohol in the two weeks prior to the study. Ten percent of those surveyed had had a blackout during that time. And 40 percent of the students said they had experienced blackouts in the previous year. A critical factor for blackouts is how much and how fast a person drinks. Another factor is whether or not the drinker has an empty stomach. It appears that blackouts are not only a problem for alcoholics.[9]

Withdrawal occurs when alcohol is taken away from an alcohol-dependent person. The term refers to the mild or severe physical and psychological responses, which can last over several days after a dependent person stops drinking alcohol. Withdrawal might start with a severe hangover, periods of insomnia, and vivid dreaming. These can be followed by mild agitation, sweating, tremors, nausea, and vomiting. Some patients may suffer seizures that happen when the nervous system recovers from the chronic depressive state induced by alcohol.[10] It is important for the safety of the alcoholic to be hospitalized when he or she goes through severe withdrawal.

Drinking and Pregnancy

It is dangerous for a pregnant woman to drink alcohol because of the potential risk to her unborn child. Fetal alcohol syndrome (FAS) is a serious condition involving physical deformities and mental retardation that occurs only in the children of alcohol users. A child born with FAS is usually small or premature with a smaller skull, eyes, upper lip, and nose. The children are often delayed in their physical and mental growth and frequently suffer from attention disorders. A less severe form of the syndrome is called fetal alcohol effect, or FAE.

An important factor that affects the kind of disability is the time during the pregnancy when a

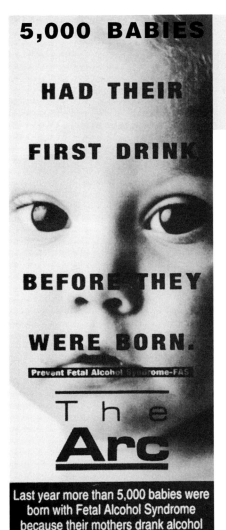

5,000 BABIES

HAD THEIR

FIRST DRINK

BEFORE THEY

WERE BORN.

Prevent Fetal Alcohol Syndrome—FAS

T h e

Arc

Last year more than 5,000 babies were born with Fetal Alcohol Syndrome because their mothers drank alcohol during pregnancy. Babies born with FAS will have mental retardation or learning problems the rest of their lives. If you're pregnant or think you might be, PLEASE don't drink. For information call The Arc today.

Fetal alcohol syndrome, or FAS, occurs in babies whose mothers drank alcohol when they were pregnant. This poster aims to educate people about FAS.

mother drank alcohol. The fetus goes through many changes during the first three months of pregnancy. Different parts of the body are formed. Even a small amount of liquor can negatively affect a baby's development and cause a lower birth weight or a higher risk of miscarriage as well as possible birth defects. Unfortunately, a woman may not know she is pregnant until it is too late to be cautious. Studies have shown that even one occurrence of binge drinking during pregnancy can result in a damaged fetus. It is recommended that women who are trying to get pregnant, as well as those who already know they are pregnant, refrain from drinking.

Alcoholism: A Disease?

As early as 1792, Dr. Benjamin Rush, a prominent American physician who was a signer of the Declaration of Independence, and Dr. Thomas Trotter, a British Royal Navy physician, defined alcoholism as a disease or medical condition. This concept took many years to become popular in the medical profession. In the 1830s, the first medical institution was opened for alcoholics. In the 1950s, the World Health Organization and the American Medical Association acknowledged that alcoholism is a medical problem. In 1960, E. M. Jellinek developed a comprehensive model of alcoholism, which described it as a progressive disease that can be arrested but not cured.

The disease model for alcoholism is based on the theory that alcoholics are physiologically different from nonalcoholics because they cannot drink in moderation. The disease model uses medical terminology. It describes physical symptoms resulting from alcohol abuse. It uses words such as *recovery* for those who give up drinking and *relapse* for those who begin to drink again. It describes the progression of the disease as deterioration occurs in the organs of the body. It acknowledges that alcoholism can be fatal. The health care system in the United States recognizes alcoholism as a disease. Treatment costs are covered under most health insurance.

Whether or not alcoholism can be classified as a

disease, medical research continues to look for a biological explanation for addiction. Scientists are studying why some people crave alcohol and others do not. Laboratory studies show that it is possible to breed rats that crave alcohol, are indifferent to it, or hate it.[11]

Alcoholism is thought to be genetic because it can often be traced down a family tree. Studies have shown that children of alcoholics run a risk of becoming addicted that is four times higher than children of nonalcoholics. Through brain scans, it is now possible to observe physical damage that has occurred over time as a person drinks excessively. There appears to be significant amounts of brain shrinkage in alcoholics as measured by autopsies and brain scans.[12] Some medical experts believe that the changes in the brain resemble those of people with other kinds of brain diseases such as Alzheimer's or Parkinson's as well as schizophrenia, clinical depression, or stroke.[13]

In addition to exploring changes in the brain caused by alcohol consumption, scientists are trying to find out if there are differences in the brains of some people that make them more susceptible to becoming alcoholics. Research is being conducted with groups of people who are known to have a high risk of becoming alcohol dependent, such as children of alcoholics.

Alcoholism: Lack of Self-Control?

Through most of history, alcohol dependency was considered a learned habit or a sign of moral depravity. There are those who believe that looking at alcoholism as a disease removes responsibility from the shoulders of the alcoholic. They admit that some people may be biologically vulnerable. But they believe that drinking excessively is about behavior and choice. Some claim that it a bad habit that can be traced to a lack of self-control. People begin to drink of their own accord, they say, then simply keep drinking until it becomes too difficult for them to stop. Opponents of the disease theory believe there are many reasons why people drink excessively. Some believe that alcoholism is a personality issue caused by people drinking to cover problems in their life. Other explanations describe alcohol abuse as a learned behavior reinforced by the wider community or an issue caused by the nature of a person's immediate environment.

Treating Alcoholism

Treatment options reflect the different beliefs about what causes alcoholism. Alcoholics Anonymous (AA) has been the primary treatment organization for many years. AA is a worldwide organization for men and women who meet regularly to help each other to stay sober. It was founded is 1935 by a New York stockbroker and an Ohio surgeon who were alcoholics. AA supports the disease model. AA members see alcohol addiction as a progressive illness. They believe that alcohol-dependent people are unable to drink in moderation. There is no cure, they say; a person can halt the progression of the disease only by stopping their drinking.

AA also has a spiritual dimension. In AA, members follow a twelve-step program. They admit they need help from a higher power to stop drinking. AA also has other support networks for families and friends (Al-Anon) and adult children of alcoholics (ACA) as well as teens who live in alcoholic families (Alateen).

There are a variety of alternative programs for people who are alcohol dependent. They can include behavior modification, education, counseling, and other techniques designed to bring about sobriety. Treatment can involve hospitalization or outpatient services. It can be individual or structured around group participation.

Sometimes people try an intervention to get help for loved ones whose lives are disrupted by excessive alcohol use. In an intervention, friends or relatives come together with the help of an alcohol counselor to confront the alcoholic and try to break through his or her denial. Ideally, the intervention results in the person going into a treatment facility.

Comorbidity

Alcoholics in treatment facilities have a high amount of comorbidity. This means that they suffer from more than one disorder. For instance, one study found that 66 percent of adolescents who misused alcohol and/or drugs also suffered from a second psychiatric disorder, such as anxiety, mood disorders, or attention problems.[14] People who have mental health disorders may use alcohol as a kind of medicine to make themselves feel better. But alcohol masks the underlying disorder, compounds the problems, and makes it difficult to diagnose and treat the patient.

Health Benefits

Studies show that moderate alcohol consumption protects adults against coronary heart disease. The Mayo Clinic recommends that adults who choose to drink should have no more than one drink per day if they are female and two drinks if they are male.[15] Drinking a small amount of alcohol decreases the risk of coronary artery disease. It lowers the risk of heart attack for people in middle age by roughly 30 to 50 percent. For those with normal blood pressure, it may reduce the risk of ischemic stroke by helping to prevent blood clots and reducing the blood vessel damage caused by fat deposits. Small amounts of alcohol may also protect against senility and Alzheimer's disease.[16] In 1995 the United States government acknowledged the health benefits of alcohol in its nutrition guidelines.

4

Alcohol
and the Law

Civilizations have always been aware that heavy drinking of alcoholic beverages causes problems. In ancient Mexico, drunkenness was considered a serious crime. It was punished with severe penalties including loss of rank, confiscation of property, and even execution.[1] Hebrew, Greek, and Roman laws show that society disapproved of drunkenness while praising the benefits of alcohol.

Problems with drinking grew when the distillation process became popular, producing stronger, more potent beverages. As the alcohol industry grew in the United States, drinking and politics became intertwined.

47

For example, there was a good deal of anti-German sentiment during World War I, including feelings against German-Americans who owned the breweries. The idea of closing these breweries was a reason for increasing support for Prohibition by the end of the war.

After the repeal of Prohibition, concerned citizens looked for new ways to keep the nation from returning to heavy drinking. The question became, How can the government help citizens control excessive drinking?

State Laws

States were expected to regulate alcohol commerce within their borders. This led to nonuniform policies across the nation, which caused a dilemma. Individual cities or counties decided whether or not they wished to sell alcohol. Many remained "dry." Some citizens could drink within their own city limits. However, drinking might be illegal in the next town. A person could be put into jail for an action that would be legal just a few blocks away.

State governments, as well as many individual cities and counties, are still free to regulate liquor trade within their own borders. Each state enacts statutes regarding the distribution, taxation, sale, and consumption of alcoholic beverages. States are also responsible for laws regarding criminal and civil liability when harm results from the consumption of alcoholic beverages.[2] State police are responsible for enforcing these laws. Although Prohibition was a national movement, the federal government today limits itself to the regulation of importation of liquor and transportation between states. It also has the power to regulate liquor sales in Washington, D.C., on military bases, and on Indian reservations.

Taxation and license requirements regulate the sale of liquor. Sometimes these methods are used to prevent the excessive use of alcohol. For instance, higher taxes on alcohol raise the prices and lower sales. Taxation is also a good way to raise revenue for the state. This is another place where politics and alcohol mix. At the beginning of Prohibition, America went through a time of economic prosperity. The Roaring Twenties brought shorter working hours and

States are in charge of regulating alcohol sales and consumption.

the introduction of numerous gadgets that made homemaking easier. But at the end of the decade, the stock market fell and the Great Depression began. When Prohibition ended and the legal alcohol industry resumed business, state and national budgets profited by the big business of alcohol sales. Sales and production of alcohol also provided jobs for citizens.

The Federal Government Intervenes

While the federal government cannot make laws for the states to follow regarding the sale and distribution of alcoholic beverages, it can use financial incentives to bring pressure on the states. This is one way to assure uniformity throughout the nation. Originally, many states adopted a minimum drinking age along with the legal age of adulthood. From 1970 through 1975, nearly all states lowered their legal age. Thirty states lowered their drinking age to eighteen.[3] They felt that eighteen-year-olds who were old enough to be required to fight in Vietnam should be old enough to legally drink alcohol.

Several studies showed that when the drinking age was lowered, there was a higher incidence of automobile accidents. Citizens' groups pressured the states to return the minimum legal drinking age to twenty-one. Some states resisted. Teens who lived in a state with a higher drinking age were driving across state lines to purchase and consume alcohol. This prompted the federal government to act.[4] The National Minimum Drinking Age Act was signed into law in 1984 by President Ronald Reagan. It required all states to raise their minimum drinking age to twenty-one within two years or lose a part of their federal highway funds. In addition, it encouraged states to pass mandatory sentencing laws to combat drunk driving.[5] By 1988, all states had adopted the new laws rather than give up their funds. According to the American Medical Association, the legislation reduced alcohol-related automobile crashes and saved the lives of well over one thousand high school and college-age youths each year.

Fatal motor vehicle accidents involving alcohol use are the leading cause of death for 15–20-year-olds in the United States. Nationwide, 40 percent of those aged sixteen to nineteen who died in alcohol-related crashes were passengers.[6] In 1997, Congress again intervened. It passed legislation requiring all states to adopt "zero tolerance" laws for drivers under the age of twenty-one by the year 1999. Even though the national minimum drinking age was twenty-one, in many states it was not specifically against the law for drivers under twenty-one to drink and drive. Zero tolerance made it illegal for people under twenty-one to drive with any measurable amount of alcohol in their bodies, since it is illegal for them to drink in the first place.

Even if they are not drinking, young drivers are twice as likely as adults to be in a fatal crash. The lack of experience, inadequate skills, poor judgment, distractions from friends, and excessive nighttime driving are factors involved in the high rate of accidents for teens.[7] One study showed that sixteen-year-old drivers get into twice as many crashes at night as eighteen- and nineteen-year-old drivers. They are six times more likely to have a nighttime crash than a forty-year-old driver.[8]

To address these discrepancies, the National Highway Traffic Safety Administration at the U.S. Department of Transportation wished to encourage states to adopt a graduated driver licensing system for new teen drivers. The idea behind the system is to phase teens into the driving task by introducing privileges gradually. New drivers have to demonstrate responsible driving behavior during each stage of licensing before advancing to the next level. Each stage includes zero tolerance for alcohol while driving.

The graduated driving license laws might vary from state to state. For instance, Washington State issues an intermediate license to sixteen-year-olds. For the first six months after they receive the license or until they reach eighteen, the holder of the license may not operate a motor vehicle that is carrying any passengers under the age of twenty who are not members of their immediate family. For the remaining period of the intermediate license, the holder may not operate a motor vehicle that is carrying more than three passengers who are under the age of twenty who are not family members. The holder may not operate a motor vehicle between the hours of 1:00 A.M. and 5:00 A.M. except when accompanied by a parent, guardian, or a licensed driver who is at least twenty-five years of age.

Teens were not the only target of new legislation. Drinking and driving is the third leading cause of death for the whole population. Every four minutes another driver in America dies as a result of drunk driving.[9] In 1998, President Bill Clinton set new standards for all drivers by promoting a national legal limit for drinking and driving. The new limit makes it illegal for an adult to operate a motor vehicle with a BAC of 0.08 percent or higher. With this law, the state does not have to prove a person is too impaired to drive. It just has to show that his or her BAC is 0.08 percent or higher. This is called a "per se" law because it stands by itself. The state does not have to prove that someone would be negatively affected by alcohol at that level. It is taken for granted. It does not mean that it is safe for a person to drive before he or she reaches the 0.08 percent limit. It simply means if a person's BAC is under this level, the state has the responsibility to prove the driver is too drunk to drive. There are financial incentives for all states to pass the 0.08 percent limit by 2007.

These new laws appear to be making America's highways safer. Total annual deaths from drinking and driving decreased from approximately 26,000 in 1982 to 17,000 in 2000, while the number of arrests for drunk drivers declined. The national goal is to reduce fatalities to no more than 11,000 by 2005.[10] However, in 2003, MADD reported

The states as well as the federal government have enacted legislation to curb drinking and driving.

that alcohol-related deaths had increased in 2002 for the third year in a row. The estimated figure for 2002 is 17,419.[11] The National Highway Traffic Safety Administration is encouraging states to require prompt, mandatory revocation or suspension of licenses when drivers refuse alcohol tests or fail them. This would allow the police and driver's licensing authorities to suspend or revoke a driver's license swiftly, without long delays while awaiting a criminal trial.[12] Many state legislatures have passed laws requiring mandatory jail time for repeated drunk driving convictions. Fines are getting larger. The lengths of license suspensions are getting longer. Citizens' groups are pushing for stronger laws and stricter penalties in an attempt to get drunk drivers off the roads.

The Costs of Alcohol Abuse

In 2000, the secretary of Health and Human Services reported to Congress that the cost of alcohol abuse and alcoholism to the United States in 1998 was around $184.6 billion. The figures include estimated costs for such items as underage drinking, health care, crime, motor vehicle accidents, and costs to the family and society for lost productivity, illness, and death.[13] Several state programs are aimed toward reducing the toll of alcohol-related incidents on society. Some states prohibit bars from serving alcohol to intoxicated patrons. Law enforcement employees and safety groups run seminars to help bartenders and waiters recognize the signs of alcohol impairment.

This helps them stop serving patrons who are on their way to becoming inebriated.

Many studies have found that raising taxes on alcohol reduces the amount sold and consumed. This especially affects young consumers, since they have less money to spend. Because alcohol is involved in a large proportion of teen crashes, raising alcohol taxes would have an effect on the number of deaths due to drunk driving. One study suggested that a dime increase in the price of beer would reduce the number of youths who drink by 11 percent.[14]

Underage Drinking

State programs aimed at controlling underage drinking focus on the sale and provision of alcohol to young people by adults. One example is beer keg laws (so called because of the popularity of parties at which beer is served in large kegs). These laws punish adults for buying and supplying beer to underage drinkers. Other laws restrict alcohol use in places youths gather, such as parks; prohibit open containers of alcoholic beverages in public; and ban alcohol from public venues such as sporting events and concerts. Social host liability laws hold adults responsible for any injury or death caused by a minor who was served alcohol in their home.

Underage drinking is one of the most violated laws in the individual states. Studies have shown how easy it is for those under twenty-one to purchase alcoholic beverages despite laws prohibiting such sales. Alcohol is obtained from family members, siblings, and often

ATTENTION

MINORS

IDENTIFICATION
IS REQUIRED

IF YOU ARE UNDER 21 YEARS OF AGE
YOU ARE SUBJECT TO A FINE OF $500
AND/OR 60 DAYS IN JAIL (1st Offense)
FOR:

1. Falsely stating your age or using false ID
   to obtain liquor.
2. Buying or attempting to buy liquor.

PLEASE
DON'T ATTEMPT
TO PURCHASE
ALCOHOLIC BEVERAGES

Establishments that sell alcohol are required to post information regarding age limits. But underage drinking remains one of the most often violated laws.

the parents themselves. Many teens have fake IDs. Laws are not uniformly enforced against those who sell alcohol to underage teens. Though thousands of minors are arrested every year for possession or consumption of alcohol, very few adults who sell or give alcohol to minors are arrested. Concern is growing about the ability of teens to buy alcohol online by giving false information that cannot be verified. The online purchase is then shipped to the home and delivered with no ID check to ensure that the recipient is twenty-one or older.

Education and Research

Millions of dollars are spent by government agencies each year for research projects about alcohol and other drugs. The National Institute on Alcohol Abuse and Alcoholism is part of the Department of Health and Human Services. Its projects help examine the causes and prevention of alcohol-related problems. Studies are used to educate citizens about the magnitude of the alcohol problem and the costs to the country of alcoholic abuse. The agency uses statistics to illustrate the health and social consequences resulting from alcohol abuse as well as to encourage new legislation and programs. Special interest groups use public service spots on television in an attempt to raise viewers' concerns. The ads spotlight problems such as drunk driving and underage drinking.

Groups such as MADD have been instrumental in changing government policies. MADD has become a watchdog for the nation. It keeps a Web site on alcohol-related laws in each state as well. It publishes a report card for the states that show the most progress in eliminating deaths by alcohol. Many of our current laws were outgrowths of MADD's vigilance in this arena. More than sixteen hundred new laws related to driving under the influence (DUI) have been passed nationwide since 1980.[15]

The Global Picture

Barbara R. Thompson, in World Vision's *Today* online magazine, says the World Health Organization calls abuse of alcoholic beverages "one of the most serious public health problems in the world." She continues to say that people all over the world suffer from alcohol-related problems such as premature deaths from accidents and violent crimes. France has a high rate of cirrhosis of the liver. Crime in Canada is linked to alcohol and illegal drugs. Russians are the leading consumers of alcohol. This is causing them to suffer a dramatic rise in alcohol-related problems.[16] Alcohol abuse is a problem in the world's developing countries as well as the world's richest nations. Teen drinking is a problem around the world. Although the drinking age varies from country to country, there is no evidence that the stricter U.S. laws and policies cause American teens to drink more. And there is no evidence that the more liberal policies in Europe correlate with lower levels of intoxication.[17]

Some believe that the citizens of the United States are in serious denial about the alcohol problem in this country. They do not understand why the nation tolerates such a high cost of alcohol abuse. Others believe that such alcohol concern is a "tempest in a teapot." The only amendment to the U.S. Constitution that repealed an earlier amendment supported every citizen's right to buy and drink alcohol. Should a few people who abuse the substance be the focus of attention when many more enjoy drinking moderately? This is a debate that goes beyond national boundaries as other countries deal with the same issues.

5

The High Cost of Alcohol Abuse

Despite the drinking laws, alcohol use by adolescents and young adults has increased steadily over the past thirty years. It is possible for young people to become alcohol dependent before it is even legal for them to drink. Moreover, a small proportion of the drinking population consumes most of the alcohol. A third of the population does not drink at all. Others are moderate drinkers. A large percentage of the population pays for the havoc that is wreaked by a very small percentage of alcohol abusers. One example is the innocent victim of a drunk driver.

59

Innocent Victims

Jeni found it hard to be the new kid in a small-town high school. No one knew that she was popular in her old school. No one knew she could dance and sing. No one had known her since kindergarten like the friends she left when she moved. She gathered her courage to try out for the elite school singing group called Swing Choir and was delighted to be one of the sixteen students accepted. Her choral partner was a tall, dark, handsome boy named Dan. He was a talented person who encouraged others and was a calm presence in the group. Jeni and Dan spent lots of time together. They performed several times as well as practiced twice a week. They shared pizzas and sodas over homework. The singing group became like a little family. The closeness fueled their performances. Audiences loved the talented youngsters.

For Jeni, it meant acceptance in her new town after a year of tremendous effort. She finally had a group of friends. In many ways, Dan made it easier for her. He was popular and well known. She was delighted to be his partner and close friend. She was no longer among strangers. Life seemed good until one Tuesday in March when her world fell apart.

Jeni received a phone call from her friend Karen. After the call, Jeni looked stunned. Her parents asked what was wrong, but she did not answer. She sat for some moments before the tears began to trickle down her cheeks. She did not move or speak. Finally, she looked up at her mother and whispered. "Dan was killed by a car. I just can't believe it."

Dan had left home early in the evening to help a friend whose car had broken down. While helping to change the tire, he was struck by a drunk driver. It was a hit-and-run. A person came forward after a few days and confessed to the crime. She was tried and sentenced for vehicular manslaughter. But Dan was gone forever. He left parents, siblings, and extended family, along with his high school friends. All those people loved him dearly. Many people suffered from his violent and sudden death.[1]

Drunk Driving

In 2002, 17,419 people in the United States were killed in crashes involving alcohol—41 percent of the people killed in all U.S. traffic crashes. According to MADD, the tragedy is that these accidents might have been prevented.[2]

Drunk driving takes its toll on the nation. But there are other costs that accompany the abuse of alcohol. Alcohol plays a significant role in all types of trauma and premature death. A large portion of nonfatal motor vehicle injuries, fires and burns, and suicides are attributed to intoxication. It is estimated that between 20 and 37 percent of all emergency-room trauma cases involve alcohol use. Also, alcohol has been estimated to be present in 50 percent of homicides.[3]

Costs to Society

The cost of alcohol abuse in dollars is heavy. Medical expenses due to alcohol abuse in 1999 were $22.6

billion. Most of this went to treat cirrhosis of the liver, HIV (often a result of unprotected sex after drinking), and trauma. The treatment of children with FAS and FAE consumed $1.2 billion. In 1995, the National Center on Addiction and Substance Abuse at Columbia University estimated that the federal government spent $11.5 billion treating the consequences of alcoholism in programs such as Medicare, Social Security, Aid to Families with Dependent Children, and food stamps.[4]

Alcohol in the workplace affects employees. It can threaten public safety, impair job performance, and result in a variety of problems—productivity

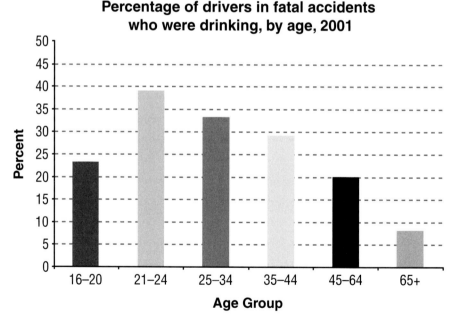

Percentage of drivers in fatal accidents who were drinking, by age, 2001

Source: U.S. Department of Transportation, National Highway Traffic Safety Administration.

loss, inefficiency, unpleasantness among workers, and poor work quality. More than 14 percent of American workers report that they drink heavily (defined as five or more drinks on five or more days in the past month).[5] School failure, absenteeism, violence, injury, child and spousal abuse, teen pregnancy, date rape, suicide, and homelessness can be attributed to alcohol abuse.

Hidden Costs

There are also hidden costs of alcohol abuse. Sometimes diseases are listed as the cause of death when alcohol was an underlying factor. All of society pays increased insurance rates and taxes because of people who are impaired. Business and industry suffer from loss of productivity when fellow workers are alcoholics. Children and spouses of alcoholics endure an undue amount of illness and upheaval in their lives.

When people abuse alcohol they impose both real and hidden costs on others. But the drinker is not the only person who pays the consequences. It is estimated that for each alcoholic, five or six other people are affected. These might include family members, friends, co-workers, employers, and agencies such as the police or social services. Exact figures are not available, but it is estimated that approximately two thirds of the population is either addicted or affected by those who are addicted.[6]

It takes an entire industry to handle problems that result from the abuse of alcohol. Large numbers of volunteers serve in soup kitchens and work with the homeless. Many people have jobs or professions that provide services to alcohol abusers. Physicians, psychiatrists, psychologists, social workers, nurses, licensed counselors, and those who work in agencies deal directly with the problem. Others, such as family members, teachers, administrators, and counselors in school districts, have daily contact with people who are affected.

Family Costs

Nowhere has alcohol abuse been more devastating than in its effect upon the family. A person with a family history of alcoholism has a significantly increased risk of becoming an alcoholic. Alcohol poses risks for members of the entire family as they struggle to cope with painful experiences. Every family works as a system. If one part of the system is not functioning, it affects the smooth working of the other parts. Not all alcoholics in families are parents. Sometimes they are grandparents, other relatives, or children.

Alcoholic families are chaotic. Life can be smooth one moment and filled with rage the next. An alcoholic member causes great havoc within the family system. This results in the breakdown of family life, with every person attempting to function the best they can in order to survive amid the anxiety, broken promises, and fear of reprisal from the alcoholic. Children of alcoholics are particularly susceptible to illness and school difficulties. Many suffer from low self-esteem, social isolation, and depression.

Those who grow up in families where one or both parents are dependent on alcohol often adapt certain ways of acting in order to survive. The research on adult children of alcoholics shows an amazing similarity in the ways they learn to function and cope. Some learn to protect the alcoholic from the outside world. They make excuses for the parent's missing work, or they try to cover up family problems caused by the drinking. Others strive hard to achieve. They want to fix things and make them right. Sometimes children seek to relieve the household tensions by acting out or being clowns. Still others become loners and isolate themselves or become problem children by turning hostile, defiant and breaking the rules.

All these ways of coping serve a purpose. They protect and hide the devastating feelings that people have when living in chaos. People function as best they can when they feel helpless to change their situation. Sometimes these ways to cope become so ingrained that they continue into adulthood. Support organizations such as Al-Anon and Alateen were founded in order to help people recover from the effects of living with problem drinking.

Why People Drink

A great many people enjoy social drinking. They might like the taste of certain drinks, feel a relief of stress, or enjoy the social atmosphere. Alcohol helps dull stressful feelings. It reduces inhibitions and helps people feel loose and happy.

It is clear that many people can handle a moderate amount of liquor. Some even can abuse liquor for a limited amount of time without becoming dependent on it. But for high-risk drinkers, even a small, enjoyable amount can be devastating. Whether or not a person is at risk for alcohol abuse, serious consequences can follow a bout of drinking. This is particularly true if the drinker gets behind the wheel of a car, engages in risky behavior without a thought for the consequences, or simply makes poor decisions that will be regretted upon sobering up. Sometimes those decisions set events in motion that the drinker will live with for the rest of his or her life.

6

The Sale
of Alcohol

The sale of alcohol is big business in America. In 2002, over 550,000 licensed retailers sold over 6 billion gallons of beer, 570 million gallons of wine, and 360 million gallons of hard liquor. This translates into well over $137 billion worth of alcohol sold.[1] The alcohol industry is a major employer and pays billions of dollars in federal, state, and local taxes each year. The alcohol industry has had a stormy history.

Early America

Even before the time of the first brewery in Massachusetts Bay in 1638, government authorities passed legislation and

67

set regulations for licensed tavern keepers on the quality and the price of beer.[2] In the mid-1700s, rum was a popular drink in the American colonies. New England sailing ships carried rum to Africa where it was exchanged for slaves. The slaves were sold in the West Indies, and the profits were used to buy molasses. The molasses was taken back to the colonies. This was called the Triangular Trade. Most of the slaves were later sold by people in the West Indies to plantation owners in America. This made the sale of rum directly responsible for much of the slavery in America. In 1808, when Congress made importing slaves to the United States illegal, the selling of rum was no longer profitable.

In 1792, there were twenty-five hundred registered commercial distilleries in America. Over the years, the government passed and repealed taxes on the alcohol industry in order to meet various monetary needs. However, after the Civil War, taxes on alcohol became a permanent part of the government's revenue system. Taxes became one way of controlling the amount of drink citizens could afford to buy.

Prohibition and After

The United States had to close nearly 178,000 saloons, over 1,200 legal breweries, over 500 legal distilleries, and an uncounted number of illegal installations when Prohibition stopped the legal sale of alcohol. Breweries and distilleries were the fifth largest industry in the country.[3] The U.S. government created a special unit to close down the makers, the sellers, and the importers of alcohol. Distillers were required to dispose of all products they had on hand when the Eighteenth Amendment was ratified. This amounted to between 58 million and 60 million gallons of beverage alcohol.[4]

When Prohibition ended, the legal sale of alcohol put the manufacturers back in business. But the newly formed industry had to contend with all the illegal liquor sellers who were still able to meet public demand. The government put together the Federal Alcohol Administration Act. This helped to create requirements and regulations and began to control the illegal sale of alcohol. Much of the control of the illegal

Even after Prohibition, the illegal manufacture of alcohol was a problem. Here a federal agent is dismantling a still found in San Francisco.

industry was in the hands of violent gangsters. The first federal gun control law was passed to control "gangster-type" weapons such as machine guns and sawed-off shotguns.

Even people who had been opposed to Prohibition did not want the previous level of problem drinking to resume. As the economy rebounded, rising prices discouraged drinking. A variety of other tactics were put into place. Although many states or counties stayed dry, others decided to use stricter measures to control the sale of distilled alcohol. Some states removed it from grocery stores and established separate liquor outlets. They imposed limits on store locations and the hours that alcohol could be sold. Liquor advertising came under close scrutiny and was restricted in many locales.

During World War II, the government offered the distilleries bonuses for converting their operations for wartime use. They provided industrial alcohol for war materials such as explosives, antifreeze, and synthetic rubber. After the war, alcohol consumption began to rise. By 1981, alcohol consumption had surpassed pre-Prohibition rates. It fell again through 1997 and began to increase again in 1998 and 1999.

Supply and Demand

Creating demand for a product is a good business practice. The alcohol industry is no exception. Making alcohol available is one of the industry's goals. Making people want to buy it is another goal. In order to keep selling alcoholic beverages, those in the beverage industry have to make sure there is a continuous supply of customers. There are many forces in the country that are working against them.

American society appears to be increasingly intolerant of the high costs of alcohol abuse. This may be a sentiment left over from the days of Prohibition. It is also because strong lobbying groups such as MADD keep the public informed about the negative consequences of excess drinking. Public service announcements are used to increase recognition of problems in society. Media attention to the harmful effects of drinking and driving has brought about public acceptance of such ideas as using designated drivers when drinking. (A designated driver is one who abstains from drinking at an event so he or she can safely drive those who drink.)

Tough drunk driving laws and underage drinking laws have an effect on the sale of liquor. Substance abuse education in schools encourages students to make healthy decisions. Colleges have instituted programs that help students to make wiser choices about the use of alcohol. As society examines its drinking habits and takes a firmer stand on alcohol abuse, it becomes a watchdog for those who would promote consumption. None of this is encouraging for the growth of the alcohol market.

Alcohol for Sale

The alcohol industry in America is composed of the vintners, or wine makers who produce products from grapes by fermentation; the brewers, or beer makers;

and the makers of distilled spirits such as whiskey, brandy, and rum. According to the World Health Organization, the United States is the world's largest beer market. It includes some of the largest brewing companies, including the world leader, Anheuser Busch. The biggest winery in the world is in California, and two of the largest whiskey producers are in the United States.[5] In order to sustain itself, the industry spends over $2 billion a year in marketing and advertising to assure that people buy its products.

For over ten years, the distillers have funded a not-for-profit organization called the Century Council. The organization develops and implements programs dedicated to fighting drunk driving and underage drinking. The International Center for Alcohol Policies (ICAP) is eight years old. It includes the beverage alcohol industry as well as other government and nongovernment organizations around the world. Their stated goal is to prevent irresponsible drinking and understand alcohol's role in the world. They help develop and review policies that affect the worldwide alcohol industry.

All three types of alcohol producers in America have voluntarily created advertising codes. These codes prohibit ads or commercials that seek to enlarge the market for alcoholic beverages. They must not attempt to persuade nondrinkers to drink or cause present drinkers to drink more. They are not to use any false or sexually provocative material in liquor ads or commercials.[6]

In addition, alcohol advertising is strictly regulated by the government. Two agencies share the responsibility. One is the Federal Trade Commission (FTC), which enforces consumer protection laws. The other is the Bureau of Alcohol, Tobacco, and Firearms (ATF). This is a branch of the United States Treasury Department that is responsible for enforcing federal laws and regulations relating to alcohol, tobacco products, firearms, explosives, and arson. In 2002, the Homeland Security Act divided the ATF into two new agencies. The Alcohol and Tobacco Tax and Trade Bureau (TTB) continues to enforce federal laws and tax codes related to the production and taxation of alcohol and tobacco products.

The United States is the world's largest market for beer. This engraving shows a nineteenth-century brewery.

The liquor industry has come under a great deal of criticism during the past several years. Concerned groups believe that it is targeting underage drinkers and minority groups and ignoring its own regulations in an attempt to encourage a potential drinking market. They say the industry rarely portrays the negative consequences of alcohol abuse.

Industry representatives disagree. They claim that they do not target new drinkers. Instead, they say, they try to make people conscious of particular brands. According to Frank Coleman of the Distilled Spirits Council, "We are a responsible industry committed to responsible advertising. We do not target our ads at underage individuals nor do we want them as our customers."[7] They are aware that irresponsible and excessive use of alcohol can lead to adverse health and social consequences. They point to the fact that there is insufficient evidence to support a relationship between advertising and either levels or patterns of drinking. Furthermore, they point to studies that show that parent and peer influence are the most powerful factors in shaping young people's beliefs and attitudes about drinking.[8]

Warning Labels

Since 1990, the United States has placed warning labels on alcoholic beverages that state the following:

> **Government Warning:** (1) According to the Surgeon General, women should not drink alcoholic beverages during pregnancy because of the risk of birth defects. (2) Consumption of alcoholic

beverages impairs your ability to drive a car or operate machinery, and may cause health problems.

When liquor is sold by the glass, rather than the bottle, warning labels are placed in the establishment that sells the products. Several other countries have followed this policy. However, research has shown that labels may be effective in raising awareness but not in changing drinking behavior.[9]

Unlike other products, alcoholic beverages do not have to list the nutritional information or ingredients on their labels.[10] For years the wine industry has tried to include information on their labels that would inform their customers about the health benefits of moderate drinking. Organizations such as the National Council on Alcoholism have called the labels "potentially dangerous."[11] The government has discouraged such action by imposing strict regulations.

Advertising

In 2000, the distilled spirits industry spent about $400 million on advertising. Most of it was for billboards and print media such as magazines. In 1996, the hard liquor industry dropped its self-imposed ban on radio and television advertising. This prompted criticism from a variety of groups. President Clinton said the move was "irresponsible." He condemned the industry for "exposing our children to such ads before they know how to handle liquor or are legally allowed to do so."[12]

In 1996, the industry began to air ads on small local stations and cable television. However, ads had

Pregnancy & Alcohol
DO NOT MIX

Drinking alcoholic beverages, including wine, coolers and beer during pregnancy can cause birth defects.

In the United States and in several other countries, warning labels are required on beverage containers as well as in establishments that sell alcohol.

not appeared on the four major networks. In December 2001, NBC became the first major network in about fifty years to agree to air advertisements for Smirnoff vodka.[13] This sparked more anger. Pressure from the American Medical Association and other interest groups was applied to the network. The following March, NBC said they would reconsider their policy and pull future ads.

Sales Targets

The beer industry spends over $900 million a year on advertising.[14] Since beer appears to be the most popular alcoholic beverage for young people, beer companies have come under harsh criticism for targeting youths. A recent study at the Center on Alcohol Marketing and Youth at Georgetown University found that beer makers delivered 45 percent more advertising to young people than to adults in magazines in 2001. The center looked at $320 million worth of alcohol advertising in magazines. It compared the information with other data on how much each magazine was looked at by teens or adults. More than half the money spent on alcohol advertising in magazines was in twenty-four magazines such as *Sports Illustrated, Rolling Stone*, and *Glamour* that had a large percentage of youthful readers.[15] One company also came under criticism in 1988 for using its Spuds McKenzie dog in ads and merchandise particularly appealing to children. Toy dogs and other "Spuds" products were sold in toy stores. The company claimed it was not targeting children to teach them about drinking. However, the merchandise soon disappeared from stores.[16]

Many alcoholic beverage ads are aired during prime time, when 31 million youngsters between the ages of two and seventeen watch television. A popular outlet for ads is sports events. According to CBS TV, 1.9 million children and 1.7 million teens watch football games.[17] The industry denies that it targets children. But it cannot deny that its ads reach millions of children who are vulnerable to advertising.

The distilled spirits industry is also under fire for its advertising of flavored alcoholic beverages popularly called alcopops. These are sweetened, carbonated fruit drinks with an alcohol content of about 5 percent. Like beer, they are malt-based products and are therefore allowed to be advertised on network television. Many have liquor-brand names, such as Smirnoff Ice and Bacardi Silver, giving the false impression that they contain hard liquors. Critics complain that the products are targeted to children and teens who may take up drinking because the sweet taste disguises the alcohol. They also criticize manufacturers for putting the liquor brand names on network television, which bans ads for hard liquor. However, the Federal Trade Commission disagreed with the critics. In June 2002, they concluded that they found no evidence that the products or their advertising targeted consumers under twenty-one years of age.

Even though targeting young people is banned in the alcohol industry, other favorite advertising venues are rock concerts and sports events or the broadcasting of sports events. Obviously, these audiences include large numbers of people younger than twenty-one. Ads appear on billboards seen in the background during sports events. Ads also appear in buses and on products popular with youths. Auto racing is an especially popular sport with teens. Beer companies sponsor races, and beer labels appear on racing paraphernalia such as shirts and model cars. Beer companies own sports stadiums and theme parks and sell products with their labels.

In 1992, the Federal Trade Commission was asked to crack down on ads that target underage consumers. Fifteen national groups signed the petition. The signers complained about the practice of manufacturers paying for their products (such as alcohol) to be shown in movies and TV shows. It is not a coincidence when a brand-name product appears in a movie. It has been paid for by a company and strategically placed for audiences to see and remember. The petition also asserts that ads linked drinking with exciting high-risk activities such as race-car driving. Ads also link drinking alcohol with pleasure without the characters suffering from blackouts, hangovers, or any other problem behaviors. The people who signed the petition

Alcopops are malt-based alcoholic beverages with a sweet, fruity taste. Critics claim that they are targeted at young people.

believed that the ads went against the standards of the FTC and the alcohol industry.[18]

Children have increasingly become Internet users. Teens go to the Web for numerous reasons such as e-mail, research, and chat rooms. One study showed that 92 percent of beer Web sites and 72 percent of distilled spirit Web sites appealed to underage audiences.[19] The content included rock music, cartoon characters, animated games, and features on fashion, sports, and music. The Center for Media Education says that the visual and interactive nature of the Web puts unprecedented power in the hands of marketers, especially to reach and influence the young. They are particularly concerned with the hundreds of Web sites that offer wine, beer, and distilled spirits for sale.[20]

Specialized Populations

One complaint about alcohol ads is that they are aimed not only at young people, but also at other specialized populations. For instance, products with lower price and higher alcohol content are targeted to low-income consumers. Products with higher prices and the image of sophistication are marketed to upper-class consumers. Ads for light drinks appeal to calorie-conscious women. Racial minorities are targeted through special promotions, ads on inner-city billboards, and in special print media. Liquor stores and billboards have higher density in lower income neighborhoods. A study in Cook County, Illinois, showed twice as many liquor stores per capita in low-income areas as in upper-middle-class or high-income areas. It also showed six times as many liquor stores in areas where there were more African Americans as in areas that were predominantly white.[21] Since the United States is a market economy, it may be fair to say that targeting special populations is an advertising technique that is unfairly blamed on the alcohol industry alone.

A 1986 four-state survey of teens by the Federal Bureau of Alcohol, Tobacco, and Firearms found a "strongly positive relationship" between exposure to advertising and a tendency to drink. A newer survey concluded that children were more likely to correlate beer consumption with the fun and good times they see on commercials than with concerns about public health.[22] However, alcohol companies contend that they are not trying to attract new customers or increase the consumption of existing customers. They continually deny that they target youths. "The distilled spirits industry takes its commitment to responsible advertising very seriously," says Peter H. Cressy, president and chief executive officer of the Distilled Spirits Council. He points to the fact that the industry's Century Council has spent more than $120 million over the past twelve years on community programs to reduce illegal underage drinking.[23]

Whether or not young people are the specific targets for advertising, it is unfortunate that children who are at great risk from alcohol for a variety of reasons may be exposed to as many as one hundred thousand beer commercials by the time they are eighteen, reports Jonathan Harris in his book *This Drinking Nation*. He goes on to say,

> A recent issue of *Adolescent Counselor Magazine* reported that a group of 8–12-year-old boys were able to name more brands of alcoholic beverages than they were U.S. Presidents. A 1987 *Weekly Reader* survey found that only 50 percent of 4th graders knew that whiskey, wine, and beer contained a drug.[24]

Advertising influences people. Advertising budgets are large and powerful. It is a fact that alcohol companies need to continue to appeal to drinkers or lose business. Perhaps they do not intend to target underage drinkers. However, there is no more promising pool of future customers than the millions of potential drinkers who turn twenty-one each year.

7

Adolescents and Alcohol

Much of the controversy about alcohol is related to the problem of teen drinking. "Alcohol is the number one drug of choice among our nation's youth," according to Karolyn Nunnallee, national president of MADD. It kills six and a half times as many young people as all other illicit drugs combined.[1] Motor vehicle accidents, homicides, and suicides are the three most common forms of death for adolescents. Motor vehicle crashes are the leading cause. Alcohol is involved in a large portion of teen homicides and suicide attempts. Suicide attempts are three to four times as high among teens who drink heavily as among those who do not drink. Drinking is often related to unexpected tragedies.

Jeremy Ballard was a twelve-year-old who weighed about one hundred pounds. He was spending the night with a friend. After watching television, the boys retrieved a bottle of vodka that they had hidden. Jeremy evidently drank most of the bottle. The next morning, he would not awaken and could not be revived. According to Washington State toxicologist Barry Logan, "three 3-ounce shots of 80-proof vodka could produce a 0.10 blood-alcohol level in a 100 pound child, which could be fatal."[2] When young teens drink, the combination of their smaller bodies and lack of tolerance can be lethal.

After drinking alcohol, people are more likely to engage in risky behavior. Teens are more likely to have sexual intercourse if they have been drinking. They are also less likely to use protection, so alcohol use is a major factor in teen pregnancy and sexually transmitted diseases. Teens who drink are more at risk for dropping out of school and using stronger illicit drugs.[3]

The Adolescent Body

Worry about underage drinking is on the rise because of a variety of concerns. Kids are trying their first drinks at younger ages. According to research by the National Institute on Alcohol Abuse and Alcoholism, the average age when youth first try alcohol is eleven years for boys and thirteen for girls. This poses several problems. Growing bodies are particularly susceptible to the toxic and addictive effects of alcohol.

Adolescents who begin drinking before fifteen years of age are four times more likely to develop an addiction than those who begin drinking at age twenty-one.[4] The amount of time it takes for a child to become addicted after beginning to drink is much shorter than the length of time it takes for an adult to become addicted. A man might take fifteen years of heavy drinking to become addicted to alcohol. A woman might take five and an adolescent a few months to a few years. This may be due, in part, to young people's undeveloped organs, particularly the brain. In addition, teens tend to drink competitively. They drink to get drunk. According to a survey conducted at Columbia University, more than 5 million high school students say that they binge drink at least once a month.[5] Boys binge drink more often than girls.

The survey shows that there are more girls drinking. They are drinking along with the boys. Unfortunately, women get drunk faster than men. Girls who match boys drink for drink might find themselves more impaired than the boys they drink with. Unfortunately, this has often made them vulnerable to unprotected sex and date rape. The researchers said that "high school students who have used alcohol at least once in their lives are seven times more likely to have had sex. They are twice as likely to have sex with four or more partners than teens who do not drink."[6] Because of the difference in response to alcohol, girls have a higher risk of driver fatality than boys at similar blood alcohol concentrations. However, they are less likely than boys to drive after drinking or to be involved in fatal alcohol-related crashes.[7]

Medical Consequences

There is increasing evidence that teens are at much greater risk than adults for serious medical consequences from alcohol use. Recent studies have shown that significant brain development happens until the age of twenty-one. Underage drinking by teenagers may inhibit that development. According to studies conducted by Sandra Brown, Ph.D., of the VA Medical Center and the University of California, San Diego, alcohol-dependent teens showed impaired memory, altered perceptions of spatial relationships, and verbal skill deficits compared to nondependent adolescents. This information coincided with similar studies showing the destruction of brain cells when heavy drinking is combined with tobacco and other drugs.[8] Again, girls may be more vulnerable than boys since they metabolize

Young people who drink run more of a health risk than adults do.

alcohol differently. Alcohol appears to interfere with normal physical and emotional development. It is not unusual for youths who drink heavily to complain of physical problems and to miss school frequently.

Adolescence is a time of turmoil. There is no other time except infancy when individual changes are so dramatic. But, unlike infants, teens are keenly aware of the changes. They cannot wish away their lack of control over their growing bodies and minds. Primary relationships become stormy as peer groups take on increasing importance. Growing up includes a long process of shifting family relationships. Teens wish for more privacy and freedom. This can cause family chaos and parental anxiety.

Change is the norm. It can be exciting. It can be disconcerting. Teens are prime candidates for seeking excitement, taking risks, and seeking peer acceptance. Young people look for quick answers and relief from the storm and stress of growing up. Too often, alcohol provides short-term relief. Alcohol becomes the drug of choice for many teens. It adds excitement and risk to a social activity.

The Effects of Alcohol

A drinking teen may feel carefree and be a bit daring or less inhibited. Alcohol may temporarily alleviate major stressors and concerns. Young teens live in the moment. They are concrete thinkers. They do not worry too much about potential dangers in an unimagined future.

In addition, teens are relatively naive and

uneducated about alcohol. For instance, they are not likely to consider the relative strengths in alcohol content when they drink. (Remember, there are various amounts of pure alcohol in different kinds of beverages—a twelve-ounce beer, a five-ounce glass of wine, and a one and a half-ounce serving of 80-proof liquor each contain the same volume of alcohol.) Many teenagers do not think about taking just a small amount of whiskey because it equals a whole can of beer. They do not realize that if they drink the same amount of whiskey as they would beer from a can, they will be drinking *eight times* the amount of pure alcohol. Teens are uneducated about how fast alcohol leaves the body. Some teens do not even know that some relatively sweet drinks, such as wine coolers, contain alcohol.

No one sets out to become addicted. Even when it takes more and more alcohol to achieve the desired effect, many young people are not particularly alarmed. They may even be unaware of their increasingly higher levels of use. If adolescents come from homes where substance abuse is the norm, alcohol may be an accepted way of handling day-to-day problems. Teens who are part of high-risk social groups may find it difficult to abstain when alcohol and drugs are an integral part of the group's social activities.

Binge Drinking and Teens

Binge drinking is a common high-risk activity. If teens binge, they often begin around thirteen years of age. They then continue bingeing during their adolescence. Binge drinking peaks from ages eighteen to twenty-two, then gradually decreases. A large number of teens drink just to get drunk or wasted.[9] Unfortunately, this activity coincides with one of the least optimum times for a growing person to drink at all. Heavy drinking and binge drinking increase the odds that a teen will use other illicit drugs, have school problems, and exhibit a wide range of delinquent behaviors. One study of 4,390 high school seniors and dropouts found that approximately 80 percent reported getting drunk, binge drinking, or drinking and driving. More than half reported that they felt sick, missed school or work, got arrested, or got into a car crash as a result of their drinking.[10]

Why Teens Drink

Peer pressure is often cited as a factor in risky behavior. Although there are peers who encourage friends to drink, more often peer pressure is an unspoken feeling on the part of the participating teen. Most teens just want to fit in to a group. If teens are not accepted into groups they covet, they will look for other people who will accept them. Friendships with adolescents who are engaged in high-risk activities will increase the odds that the teen will get caught up in the same activities.

There are a variety of reasons why some teens get involved in drinking more than others. A teen who is low on impulse control may indulge in high-risk drinking because he or she is in the wrong place at the wrong time. Teens with low self-esteem are highly critical of themselves. Sometimes they make errors in judgment that set them on a particular course of action. Instead of correcting the problem, they continue to go down a destructive path. This is especially true when teens have sex. Sometimes teens believe that alcohol makes sex better. However, those who have sex under the influence of alcohol often regret it later.

A serious problem occurs when teens combine alcohol and other drugs. The combination of different drugs may have an effect that renders one or the other drugs much more powerful than usual. This can be lethal to the user. Alcohol potentiates other drugs—that is, it multiplies their effects. An overdose can be the result.[11] Unfortunately, the use of alcohol often dulls the immediate ability to make practical and wise decisions.

Risk and Protective Factors

Why do some teens drink more than others? Studies show a variety of risk and protective factors that make a teen more or less likely to drink. Adolescents who come from alcoholic homes are four times more likely to become early drinkers. Teens who come from unhappy or abusive situations may drink earlier, and those who come from homes with few boundaries and few rules, such as curfews, are more at risk. On the other hand, teens who come from homes where there are clear and consistent boundaries, close relationships with parents, and consequences for breaking the rules are less likely to begin drinking early.

Older siblings can positively or negatively influence their sisters and brothers. Teens who hang out with friends who use alcohol tend to drink more. There may be some particular times when risk factors are higher than others. Transitioning into new schools or neighborhoods and going from middle school to high school or from high school to college—all these are times of high stress. Some school environments are more risky than others. This is especially true when

Teens who are close to their parents are less likely to begin drinking at young ages.

alcohol is more readily available and more students are drinking. Disorders such as depression or attention problems might make a teen more vulnerable. A teen who is very impulsive might act first and think later. Clearly, tightening up on laws regarding drinking age and drinking and driving have curbed underage drinking to some degree. Many teens refuse to take the chance of having their license revoked.

One strong risk factor is the beliefs that teens have gathered over their lifetime. Those who come from homes that have favorable attitudes toward drinking and the expectation that teens will experiment are more likely to drink. Adolescents who believe that alcohol will bring them pleasure and make life wonderful will begin to drink earlier. This is one reason why the alcohol industry gets so much criticism about its campaigns. Young people watch thousands of ads or movies where alcohol is portrayed as a wonderful way to relax, meet glamorous people, and have a good time. This instills a drinking expectation. Then, if young people with such an expectation find that alcohol is relaxing and gives them a buzz, those feelings are reinforced. This is why the industry is criticized for not shattering the image by telling the rest of the story about alcohol—such as the negative effects that drinking can bring into a child's life.

Cultural Differences

According to a survey of high school students conducted by the National Institute of Alcohol Abuse and Alcoholism, teen alcohol use varies among racial groups. A 1997 report looked at African-American, Hispanic, and white youths. African Americans reported the lowest rate of drinking alcohol and getting drunk at grade levels eight, ten, and twelve. Interestingly, Hispanic youngsters had similar rates to whites at grade eight, but by grade ten, white students began to get drunk more. By grade twelve, nearly twice as many whites as Hispanics reported getting drunk. This figure might be skewed by the fact that the dropout rate for Hispanic students is higher than that for whites. Other studies show a very low rate of use among Asian students. It is difficult to get an accurate picture of American Indian students. The survey samples do not give enough information to make generalizations.[12] Because there are so many different American Indian tribes and languages, it would be safe to say that there are many different views of drinking alcohol.

College-Age Drinking

Some of the heaviest drinking for adolescence happens between ages seventeen and twenty. The NIAAA survey showed that more than half of twelfth graders report having had one drink in the past thirty days, and more than one third reported that they had been drunk.[13] This is also confirmed by the College of Alcohol Studies at Harvard University. They conducted surveys of 119 four-year colleges during 1993, 1997, 1999, and 2001. In 2001, they found that approximately 44 percent of college students reported binge drinking. This is similar to studies from other years.[14] The transition from high school to college is often associated with increased alcohol use. Leaving home is a major life transition that causes anxiety and stress. Most students are free from parental restrictions for the first time in their lives. Many have little information about drinking responsibly. It may be the first time that they experience the pressure of serious academic competition. Often students enter college believing that drinking alcohol is a necessary component of the social scene. However, students find that it becomes difficult to maintain an academic standing and drink heavily. Heavy drinkers experience a variety of problems both on and off their college campus. These can include trouble with the police, property damage, injuries, drinking and driving, sexual aggression, and rape. Sororities and fraternities have often been in the news because of their heavy alcohol use. Stories of hazing where students are forced to drink large quantities of alcohol have been reported for years.

Nineteen-year-old Daniel Reardon was a freshman at the University of Maryland at College Park when he died from excessive use of alcohol. He drank until he was unconscious during a party at his fraternity house. He was taken by ambulance to the hospital. Tests showed a blood alcohol level of 0.5 percent. Correspondent Susan Dentzer, who covered this story for a PBS news article, reports that alcohol consumption and resulting accidents are responsible for approximately fourteen hundred college student deaths a year, according to a federally funded study.[15]

Morgan Luce and Matt Greenstreet are both freshmen at Western Washington University in Bellingham, Washington. They made a choice to live in a dorm that has a substance-free floor. Matt's father, a volunteer fireman, had told his family about the many times he was called out on emergencies and witnessed accidents due to drinking and driving. Matt decided that he could minimize the risk of being in a car with a drunk driver by associating with students who choose not to drink. Morgan wanted to live with students who shared similar ideals. She says, "We also tend to find our own fun on many a Saturday night that is much more memorable in the morning and for weeks to come."[16]

College students who do not participate in drinking at all, or drink little, say that they experience a variety of secondhand effects from the drinking of fellow students. They report their sleep or their studies being interrupted, property damage, and verbal, physical, or sexual violence.[17] College binge drinking also negatively affects the surrounding neighborhoods. Many college students live in off-campus locations. They drive on off-campus streets and buy their products at local markets. Clearly, problem drinking on campuses has an effect on entire communities.

Many colleges have had success with a campus-based program designed to change student perceptions of drinking norms. The program, called "Harm Reduction," has been tried by several colleges and universities in the past fifteen years. After trying a variety of prevention efforts with little success, Northern Illinois University (NIU) decided to rethink its approach. In a campus survey, the university administration found that students believed that more than two thirds of the students on campus were binge drinkers, though fewer than half of the students actually were. It was decided that the overestimation of binge drinking actually became a strong motivation to drink.

The campaign flooded the student body with messages on campus that corrected the wrong assumptions about drinking rates. Newspaper ads and speakers carried the message that most NIU students drank five or fewer drinks when they partied. They did not focus on individual drinking behaviors. Instead, they focused on changing student perceptions of campus drinking in general. The message conveyed moderate drinking norms. They found that their media campaign significantly reduced binge drinking on campus over six years by about 35 percent. This also included 31 percent fewer alcohol-related injuries to self and 54 percent fewer injuries to others.[18]

The University of Arizona (UA) adopted a similar program in 1995. Like NIU, they also worked to change misperceptions on campus. By educating students, UA saw a 22 percent decline in heavy drinking within twenty-four months and 29 percent within three years.[19]

These social norms programs have gained popularity in recent years. But a 2003 study at the Harvard School of Public Health questions their effectiveness. In fact, the study concluded that the programs make drinking seem "normal" and do not emphasize the negative consequences of heavy drinking. They indicated that enforcing the minimum-age drinking laws and limiting the access and cheap price of alcohol around colleges would be more effective.[20]

Some Ideas for Teens

There are a variety of things a teen can do to avoid the devastating effects of alcohol. The most obvious is not to drink. Drinking under age twenty-one is against the law. It is extremely important to recognize the dangers of binge drinking for young adolescents.

When teens keep their eye on their long-term goals, they may be more likely to think through their

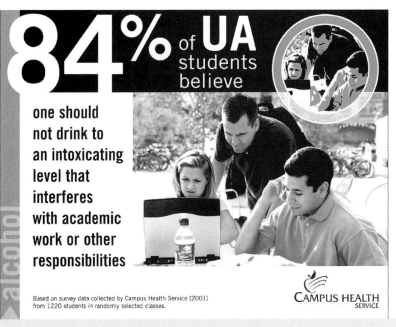

84% of UA students believe

one should not drink to an intoxicating level that interferes with academic work or other responsibilities

Based on survey data collected by Campus Health Service (2001) from 1220 students in randomly selected classes.

CAMPUS HEALTH SERVICE

At the University of Arizona, posters like this were displayed to inform students that binge drinking is not the norm.

short-term behavior. Susan was a thirteen-year-old who told her counselor, "I should have never gone over to his house. Once I made that mistake, I had difficulty saying no. Drinking and sex followed. I need to remember what lines to draw. I need to remember not to cross those lines."[21] Those lines might be avoiding unsupervised situations, not getting into a car with someone who has been drinking, or not running around with friends who continue to drink. If teens remove themselves from danger zones, chances are they can remove themselves from danger.

Some recent studies show programs that teach good skills are more effective in the long term than those that tell teens not to drink. When teens are taught refusal skills and good communication skills, they are more able to keep their friends while keeping out of potential trouble. Parents can often be used as scapegoats. "I would really love to go to the party with you, but my parents say that I can't. How about if you come over to my house instead?" or "I really want to go to Sarah's party, but my dad says I can't. Maybe we can do something on Saturday." Saving face is important for teens.

Some families have passwords that teens can use when they find themselves in a compromising position. Joanne Johnson, an intervention specialist for the Bellingham School District in Washington State, had a secret code with her girls when they were growing up. If they called and said they had a migraine, she would pick them up from any activity, no questions asked. That was a code word for, "Come get me. I need to get out of this place."[22]

Prevention and Treatment Programs

Most teens have experienced prevention programs in their schools. These programs seem to be more effective among low-risk students than with those who begin drinking very young. Studies show that existing prevention programs have been minimally effective in reducing risk.[23] Open-ended programs that elicit discussion and debate as well as building social skills appear to be better accepted.

There are over three thousand specialized treatment programs for youths addicted to alcohol. A variety of approaches have been used with teens, such as the AA twelve-step model, behavior modification, and family therapy. The relapse rate for teens is very high. There are many variables that determine success after treatment, including the length of time in treatment, how long a teen has been drinking, whether or not alcohol is masking or causing a separate disorder, and whether treatment has been entered voluntarily. Medication for addiction is seldom used with adolescents with alcohol disorders, although it is often used for accompanying conditions.[22]

Teens and alcohol have been together for as long as history has been written. The story of alcohol misuse among teens is especially sad because so many tragedies could have been prevented. As long as teens needlessly lose their lives to alcohol misuse, there will continue to be a need for education, prevention programs, and places such as treatment centers where they can heal.

8

Current
Alcohol Issues

Everyone seems to have a strong opinion about the recreational use of alcohol. About 30 percent of adults do not drink at all. Many others enjoy safe and responsible drinking. A small percentage of adults are alcohol abusers, and some teens drink illegally. American adults have a legal right to drink, to serve, and to sell alcohol. Individual states have the authority to decide how much to restrict that right. During the past several years, the federal government has increasingly intervened in this issue by threatening to withhold highway funds in order to pressure states into passing new laws. Some people are angry

100

that the federal government is involved in an issue which, by law, belongs to the states.

Responsible people generally understand the need for laws that reduce underage drinking and disorderly and dangerous behavior. However, some question the amount of government involvement in the lives of citizens. They ask why the federal government needs to be involved at all. After all, they say, only a small fraction of people abuse alcohol. Some people wonder whether the statistics cited by politicians and policy makers are simply political rhetoric to gain votes by appealing to citizen concerns. They think that people should take responsibility for their individual choices, and there should be less government intervention.

There are Americans who consider alcohol to be a dangerous drug. They are astounded that a potentially toxic substance that has wrecked so many lives is not illegal like marijuana or cocaine. They believe that the costs of alcohol abuse are a major concern in the country. The passing of laws and economic leverage are ways to curtail some of the damage. The government should protect its citizens. They believe that curtailing a few rights is a small price to pay.

It is widely agreed that alcohol abuse does not just affect the problem drinker, but all of society. Does a citizen have the right to drink irresponsibly? Who protects the victims against the people who make poor choices? Who protects the rights of a person to live in a society free from harm? Can those rights be protected without the interference of government? These are questions at the heart of a democracy.

Interest Groups

The special interest groups involved with alcohol are politically powerful. They have considerable influence on the policies developed in the United States. The alcohol industry is a major contributor to the nation's economy. The distilled spirits industry alone generates $95 billion to the U.S. economy annually. It employs over 1.3 million people in the manufacture, distribution, and sale of distilled spirits. Jobs within the industry account for more than $28 billion in wages.[1] The beer industry employs close to a million people and pays almost $14 billion in federal, state, and local taxes.[2] These industries make up a strong political lobby.

The U.S. government spends billions of dollars to fight alcohol abuse. The National Institute of Alcohol Abuse and Alcoholism costs the taxpayers over $400 million per year. The Substance Abuse and Mental Health Services Agency, which is part of the Department of Health and Human Services, costs $3 billion. Working alongside government agencies are professional groups such as the American Medical Association, university research organizations such as the Alcohol and Drug Abuse Institute at the University of Washington (ADAI) and the National Center on Addiction and Substance Abuse (CASA), as well as organizations and advocacy groups such as Alcoholics Anonymous and Mothers Against Drunk Driving.

These are just a few organizations that are a force for political change in America. The topic of alcohol in America sets a variety of complex forces into action and sustains astronomical budgets.

An International Issue

Alcohol abuse is not confined to the United States. Most of the same issues are debated in countries all over the world. The International Center for Alcohol Policies (ICAP) was founded in 1995 in order to bring together government and nongovernment organizations, the alcohol industry, and the scientific and public health communities to prevent irresponsible drinking and achieve a better understanding of alcohol's role in the world.[3] ICAP is sponsored by the major beverage alcohol producers. There are divisions of interests between the beverage producers and others who disagree with their stance on issues such as moderate drinking. Some may believe that the organization does not speak for all interested parties. However, ICAP attempts to speak to the following major issues facing countries today in the field of alcohol abuse.

Economic Costs

All countries where alcohol is consumed have concerns about alcohol abuse. How that abuse is defined is not always a topic of agreement. Studies estimating the economic costs of alcohol misuse are conducted in a few countries that have relatively good data systems and appropriate expertise, such as Australia, Canada, and the United States. There are a variety of factors involved in estimating those costs. They include such things as the impact on the costs of production for companies with workers who abuse alcohol. They also include resources spent on treatment, prevention, research, and law enforcement due to alcohol abuse. These studies are not always consistent due to the use of different methods and the lack of accurate data. Efforts are under way to improve the studies and arrive at a greater international consensus concerning the methods used to obtain data. Accurate studies allow countries to target problems, develop appropriate policies on alcohol use, and institute programs to reduce harm.[4]

Gender Differences

One emerging issue is the difference in drinking patterns between males and females. As previously stated, a woman's body handles alcohol differently from a man's body. Prejudice and stereotyping have often colored opinions on women's drinking in the past. Even today, many countries attach a greater stigma to heavy drinking by females than to males. In most societies, women are less likely to drink or to consume as heavily as males. There is a question as to whether the gap is lessening because women are drinking more or because men are drinking less. There is a worldwide consensus that drinking by pregnant women is harmful and contributes to such ill effects as fetal alcohol syndrome. It is also generally agreed that increased drinking by women makes them more vulnerable to alcohol abuse and consequences such as unwanted sexual behavior. This is an area that will continue to be studied.[5]

Health Labeling

The United States has been at the forefront of placing health labels on alcoholic beverage containers. Including nutritional information is consistent with other food products. It enables the consumer to understand the risks and to make appropriate choices. However, those who disagree believe that people already know the risks of excessive drinking, and they say that labels are too small to include all the pertinent information. Some say it is not fair or accurate to include only the liabilities of drinking.

Treatment Options

People who enter treatment for alcohol abuse vary in their ability to get clean and sober. The debate involves the nature of treatment options. Which treatment works best? There are opposing views on the underlying causes of alcohol problems. The school that favors the "disease model" prescribes abstinence as the best intervention. Other treatments may favor "controlled drinking." Options include a variety of therapies and approaches. However, most treatment facilities in the United States still favor the traditional abstinence-only approach for alcoholics.[6]

Drinking and Driving

There is considerable agreement that societies have to address the issue of drinking and driving. There are worldwide discrepancies in permissible BAC levels and enforcement. The United States has the highest permissible BAC levels, with four states allowing 0.10 percent BAC as the threshold for impaired driving.

However, as earlier stated, all states must conform to the 0.08 percent standard by 2007 or risk losing federal highway funding. Nine countries have set BAC levels at 0.08 percent, while twenty-seven countries use 0.05 percent as their legislated BAC. Norway and Sweden use 0.02 percent. Eight countries do not allow any traces of alcohol in a driver's blood. Russia indicates that "drunkenness" is the standard. There is little agreement regarding blood alcohol levels. This might stem from the fact that the BAC charts show a difference in impairment between males and females and are based on the differences in body weight. There is also a great deal of variety on enforcement and punishment between countries.[7]

This sign in Washington State gives a message about the costs of drinking and driving.

Biological Vulnerability and Harm Reduction

Two other issues debated internationally are the biological vulnerability to alcohol abuse and the appropriate approach to reducing harmful consequences. There seems to be no disagreement that some individuals are more vulnerable to alcohol and the severe physical reactions that result from drinking. There is a wide agreement that some drinkers are biologically vulnerable because of genetics, health conditions, gender, and age. It is also agreed that heavy and chronic alcohol consumption puts all people at risk. There are differences of opinion, however, on acceptable strategies for reducing risk to different groups.

The two main ideas differ in the approach from the drinker to the drinking. The first strategy is based on the premise that abstinence is the most effective response to prevent problem drinking or alcohol dependence. The harm reduction approach lists a set of practical strategies that help to reduce negative consequences of alcohol use. It promotes patterns of drinking that are consistent with generally healthy lifestyles. Harm reduction accepts alcohol use and works to minimize the harmful effects rather than ignore or condemn them. These different approaches are the source of heated debates.[8]

Advertising

A hot issue is whether or not the alcohol industry can regulate itself adequately when it comes to advertising. Internationally, the regulation of advertising varies widely between countries. Thirty-nine countries have statutes that regulate advertising, nineteen have systems of industry self-regulation, and twenty-four countries use a combination of the two. Twenty countries have no official means of regulating advertising, and eight ban advertising.[9] Advertising is designed to make consumers want to buy. It may be impossible for the alcohol industry to advertise their products and meet criteria set by their own or governmental standards. How is it possible to tell whether or not a flashy ad is directed toward a twenty-five-year-old drinker or a teen? How can children be kept from watching beer commercials aimed at adults? Even if the industry does not target youths, it is impossible to keep youths separate from advertising.

Binge Drinking

Binge drinking has gained attention worldwide because of the harmful and potentially deadly effects on young people. There is still some difference of opinion about what constitutes binge drinking. It is commonly referred to by the number of drinks consumed at a particular occasion. However, that does not define the size or strength of the drinks or the length of the occasion. Another definition refers to consuming alcohol to the point of intoxication. This is often a solitary and self-destructive activity that lasts up to several days and involves loss of control. It is also referred to as heavy episodic drinking.[10] Binge drinking is a public health concern. A more consistent definition would allow a more uniform approach to the problem.

Drinking Age

One of the most controversial questions in the area of alcohol regulation is the debate over the legal drinking age. The legal age for purchase and/or consumption of alcohol varies considerably from country to country, from twenty-one years of age in the United States, Malaysia, Ukraine, and Korea to sixteen years of age in Italy, France, Belgium, and Spain. There are countries such as China, Portugal, and Thailand that currently have no established legal limits. Usually the various national laws relate to drinking age limits for settings outside of the home. In some countries, purchase limits are based on the alcohol content or type of beverage. Distilled beverages are often treated differently from beer and wine.

Lately there has been more consideration given to creating a more uniform drinking age across geographical boundaries. This may be difficult, given that drinking age limits are often the product of cultural views about alcohol and the role it plays in the society. They also reflect a society's attitude toward young people drinking.

In America, the issue has been confused by the changes in legal drinking age over the years in various states. It entered the spotlight again when President Bush's nineteen-year-old daughter, Jenna Bush, was arrested twice in less than a month for consuming alcohol and using a fake identification card. Many citizens feel that it is unfair that eighteen-year-olds enjoy all the legal aspects of being an adult. They can get married and vote. But they cannot buy alcoholic beverages.

The legal drinking age varies from country to country; some countries have no legal limits. Recently it has been suggested that a more uniform legal drinking age be established.

However, interest groups point to lives saved on the highway as being a good reason to keep the drinking age at twenty-one. Since drinking statistics show that many begin drinking at a younger age, more research is needed on whether the laws keep the majority of young people alcohol-free or cause them to react and drink more.

The Future

What is the face of the future? A number of technological advances in the field of alcohol research have been made. Researchers have identified some brainwave patterns that are associated with alcoholism. These may help researchers identify people who are at risk. One priority for researchers is to find the genes that are involved in alcoholism vulnerability. They are hoping that the map of the human genome will lead the way to this discovery. Experiments with mice show that researchers can alter the genetic structure and control preference for alcohol consumption. It may be possible in the future to identify every gene and its protein that affect alcohol-related behavior.[11]

For many years the drug Antabuse was used with adult alcoholics. Antabuse made people sick when they drank. The idea was to make them feel sick when they even thought about drinking. The drug naltrexone has recently been approved by the FDA. It is being tried in treatment centers. The drugs target the neurons involved with craving. Topiramate, an antiseizure drug, has been used in a study over three months with good results. It also reduced the craving for alcohol.[12] Learning more about the physical nature of dependence provides tools to design interventions. Vast research throughout the country has brought about methods to review the nation's policies and laws and to plan new treatment and design prevention strategies.

Alcohol abuse may be an age-old subject, but it is being looked at with modern international technology and research. It is the hope of today's research that people will be able to enjoy drinking alcohol without becoming addicted. A perfect world would have no deaths from drunk driving or disease from alcohol misuse. Healthy citizens would have free choice to drink or to abstain without suffering from the poor decisions of others regarding alcohol.

Chapter Notes

Chapter 1. Tyler and Lani

1. Aubrey Cohen, "Tyler DuHart Lived When 3 Friends Died, But Survival Hasn't Been Easy," *The Bellingham* (Washington) *Herald*, February 24, 2002, p. A1.

2. Washington State Patrol, *Police Traffic Collision Report*, March 27, 1999.

3. Kathryn Blair essay, November 1999.

4. J. Vincent Peterson, Bernard Nisenholz, and Gary Robinson, *A Nation Under the Influence* (Boston, Mass.: Pearson Education, 2003), p. 64.

5. Lloyd D. Johnston, Patrick M. O'Malley, and Jerald G. Bachman, *Monitoring the Future: National Survey Results on Drug Use, 1975–2001*, Volume I: Secondary School Students, Table 2-2 (Washington, D.C.: U.S. Department of Health and Human Services: National Institutes of Health, 2002).

6. Ibid., p. 22.

7. Cohen.

8. Personal interview with Lelenya Bartlett, May 20, 2003.

Chapter 2. The History of Alcohol

1. "A Short History of Beer," *Beer World*, n.d., <http://www.dailyglobe.com/beer/hist.html> (October 9, 2002).

2. Bert L. Vallee, "Alcohol in the Western World: A History, Part 2," *Beekman Wines & Liquors*, n.d., <http://www.beekmanwine.com/prevtopy.htm> (October 2, 2002).

3. "Now on Display . . . World's Oldest Known Wine Jar," *Worldwide Research from the University of Pennsylvania Museum of Archaeology and Anthropology*, n.d.,

<http://www.upenn.edu/museum/News/wine.html> (October 3, 2002).

4. Caroline Seawright, "Ancient Egyptian Alcohol," *Tour Egypt Monthly*, April 1, 2001, <http://www. touregypt.net/magazine/mag04012001/magf2.htm> (October 3, 2002).

5. Ibid.

6. Vallee.

7. "Social and Cultural Aspects of Drinking," *Social Issues Research Center*, n.d., <http://www.sirc.org/publik/ drinking_origins.html> (October 2, 2002).

8. R. Vashon Rogers, Jr., *Intoxicating Liquors* (New York: Weed, Parsons and Company, 1881), p. 37.

9. Ibid., p. 24.

10. Donald W. Goodwin, *Alcoholism: The Facts* (New York: Oxford University Press, 1998), p. 5.

11. J. Vincent Peterson, Bernard Nisenholz, and Gary Robinson, *A Nation Under the Influence* (Boston, Mass.: Pearson Education, 2003), p. 18.

12. "A Short History of Beer."

13. Michael Windle, *Alcohol Use Among Adolescents* (Thousand Oaks, Calif.: Sage Publications, 1999), p. 3.

14. "A Short History of Beer."

15. "Cider," *History of Alcohol in America 20-20 Site*, n.d., <http://www.2020site.org/drinks/cider.html> (October 2, 2002).

16. Michael Pollan, *The Botany of Desire* (New York: Random House, 2001), pp. 6–9.

17. Jonathan Harris, *This Drinking Nation* (New York: Four Winds Press, 1994), pp. 29–30.

18. Catherine Gilbert Murdock, *Domesticating Drink: Women, Men, and Alcohol in America 1870–1940* (Baltimore: The Johns Hopkins University Press, 1998), p. 17.

19. "Where Did Evangelical Objections to Smoking and Drinking Come From?" *Christian History, Christianity Today*, July 12, 2002, <http://www.christianitytoday. com/history/features/ask/2002/jul12.html> (October 3, 2002).

20. Murdock, p. 39.

21. "Medicinal Alcohol: Temperance & Prohibition," *Ohio State University*, n.d., <http://www.cohums. ohio-state.edu/history/projects/prohibition/Medicinal_ Alcohol.htm> (October 8, 2002).

22. Harris, p. 97.

23. Alice Fleming, *Alcohol: The Delightful Poison* (New York: Delacorte Press, 1976), p. 84.

24. Harris, p. 95.

25. Murdock, p. 172.

26. Peterson, Nisenholz, and Robinson, p. 15.

27. Harris, p. 120.

Chapter 3. Alcohol and the Human Body

1. Peter M. Monti, Suzanne M. Colby, and Tracy A. O'Leary, eds., *Adolescents, Alcohol, and Substance Abuse: Reaching Teens Through Brief Interventions* (New York: The Guilford Press, 2001), p. 193.

2. Ibid., p. 194.

3. Ibid., p. 196.

4. J. Vincent Peterson, Bernard Nisenholz, and Gary Robinson, *A Nation Under the Influence* (Boston, Mass.: Pearson Education, 2003), p. 24.

5. Ibid., p. 28.

6. Ibid., p. 28.

7. Monti, Colby, and O'Leary, p. 201.

8. "From Genes to Geography: The Cutting Edge of Alcohol Research," *NIAAA: Alcohol Alert*, July 2000, <http://www.niaaa.nih.gov/publications/aa48.htm> (October 31, 2002).

9. Mike Foley, "Student Drinking Leads to Blackouts," *The Bellingham* (Washington) *Herald*, May 1, 2003, p. C1.

10. Peterson, Nisenholz, and Robinson, p. 23.

11. Eric Newhouse, *Alcohol: Cradle to Grave* (Center City, Minn.: Hazelton Foundation, 2001), p. 30.

12. Peterson, Nisenholz, and Robinson, p. 39.

13. Ibid., p. 98.

14. Monti, Colby, and O'Leary, p. 276.

15. "Alcohol and Your Health: Weighing the Pros and Cons," *MayoClinic.com*, August 22, 2002, <http://www.mayoclinic.com/invoke.cfm?id=SC00024> (October 31, 2002).

16. Ibid.

Chapter 4. Alcohol and the Law

1. R. Vashon Rogers, Jr. *Intoxicating Liquors* (New York: Weed, Parsons and Company, 1881), p. 35.

2. "State Alcohol Law," *Alcohol Epidemiology Program*, 2000, <http://www.epi.umn.edu/enacted> (November 4, 2002).

3. Alex Koroknay-Palicz, "Legislative Analysis for the National Minimum Drinking Age Act," n.d., <http://www.asfar.org/zine/5th/cover.html> (November 1, 2002).

4. "The Minimum Legal Drinking Age: Facts and Fallacies," *American Medical Association*, n.d., <http://www.ama-assn.org/ama/pub/article/3566-3640.html> (September 16, 2002).

5. Koroknay-Palicz.

6. "Did You Know . . .," *MADD Online*, n.d., <http://www.madd.org/stats/0,1056,1807,00.html> (September 30, 2002).

7. National Highway Traffic Safety Administration, U.S. Department of Transportation, "Graduated Driver Licensing System," *State Legislative Fact Sheet*, April 2002.

8. Dick Doanne and Kathy Griffith, "The Crash Involvement of Young Novice Drivers: The Problem and a Solution," Washington Traffic Safety Commission, October 2000, p. 7.

9. J. Vincent Peterson, Bernard Nisenholz, and Gary Robinson, *A Nation Under the Influence* (Boston, Mass., Pearson Education, 2003), p. 54.

10. "A History of MADD's Policies," *MADD Online*, n.d., <http://www.madd.org/aboutus/0,1056,4077,00.html> (November 1, 2002).

11. "Total Traffic Fatality vs. Alcohol Related Traffic Fatality," *MADD Online: Stats and Resources*, July 17, 2003, <http://www.madd.org/stats/0,1056,1298,00.html> (December 15, 2003).

12. National Highway Traffic Safety Administration, U.S. Department of Transportation, "Administrative License Revocation (or Suspension): Key Facts," *State Legislative Fact Sheets*, January 2001, <http://www. nhtsa.dot.gov/people/outreach/stateleg/adminlicense. htm> (November 3, 2002).

13. "NIAAA Special Report to United States Congress on Alcohol and Health," *National Institute on Alcohol Abuse and Alcoholism*, June 2000, <http://www.niaaa. nih.gov/publications/10report/intro.pdf> (October 20, 2002).

14. Michael Windle, *Alcohol Use Among Adolescents* (Thousand Oaks, Calif.: Sage Publications, 1999), p. 81.

15. "Drunk Driving Penalties," *What You Need to Know About . . . Alcoholism/Substance Abuse*, n.d., <http://alcoholism.about.com/library/weekly/aa990903. htm?terms=drinking+age+laws> (October 29, 2002).

16. Barbara R. Thompson, "Global Binge: A Report on Alcohol Abuse Worldwide," *World Vision's Today Magazine*, December 1996, <http://www.worldvision. org/worldvision/mag.nsf/217alc6d85845c0085256475 000ccf4b.html> (November 20, 2002).

17. "Justice Department Releases First Time Comparison Data on European and U.S. Youth Drinking Rates and Problems," *Parent-Teen.com*, July 19, 2001, <http://www.parent-teen.com/newsreleases2001/ eurodrinking.html> (November 2, 2002).

Chapter 5. The High Cost of Alcohol Abuse

1. Personal interview with Jennifer Craswell, June 23, 2003.

2. "Total Traffic Fatality vs. Alcohol Related Traffic Fatality," *MADD Online: Stats and Resources*, July 17, 2003, <http://www.madd.org/stats/0,1056,1298,00. html> (December 15, 2003).

3. "Alcohol and Trauma: Alcohol Alert from NIAAA," *What You Need to Know About . . . Alcoholism/Substance Abuse*, n.d., <http://alcoholism.about.com/library/ blnaa03.htm> (October 29, 2002).

4. Eric Newhouse, *Alcohol: Cradle to Grave* (Center City, Minn.: Hazelton Foundation, 2001), p. 156.

5. Ibid., p. 157.

6. Jonathan Harris, *This Drinking Nation* (New York: Four Winds Press, 1994), p. 130.

Chapter 6. The Sale of Alcohol

1. "Alcoholic Beverage Sales Up In 2002," *Modern Brewery Age*, March 10, 2003, *Looksmart*, <http://www.findarticles.com/cf_0/m3469/10_54/99207252/pl/article.jhtml> (December 23, 2003).

2. G. Thompson, *American Beer: Glimpses of Its History and Description of Its Manufacture* (Chapter 1: New England), United States Brewers' Association, 1909, <http://brewery.org/librar/ambeer/AB_02.html> (December 23, 2003).

3. Jonathan Harris, *This Drinking Nation* (New York: Four Winds Press, 1994), p. 86.

4. "AFT History," *Bureau of Alcohol, Tobacco and Firearms*, n.d., <http://www.fas.org/irp/agency/ustreas/atf/hist.htm> (November 12, 2002).

5. J. Vincent Peterson, Bernard Nisenholz, and Gary Robinson, *A Nation Under the Influence* (Boston, Mass.: Pearson Education, 2003), p. 14.

6. Harris, p. 139.

7. Frank Coleman, Distilled Spirits Council, "The Alcohol Industry on Record," *Center on Alcohol Marketing and Youth: Fact Sheets*, July 16, 2002, <http://camy.org/factsheets/index.php?FactsheetID=3> (December 1, 2002).

8. "Industry Views on Beverage Advertising and Marketing, with Special Reference to Young People," prepared for the World Health Organization by the International Center for Alcohol Policies, n.d., <http://www.icap.org/pdf/who_paper_annexed.pdf> (November 28, 2002).

9. "Health Message Labeling," *International Center for Alcohol Policies*, <http://www.icap.org/international/hmlabeling.html> (November13, 2002).

10. Peterson, Nisenholz, and Robinson, p. 26.

11. Jacob Sullum, "On Wine Labels, Truth is No Defense," *The Washington Times*, March 11, 2003, <http://www.washtimes.com/commentary/20030311-25206984.htm> (May 9, 2003).

12. "Clinton Denounces Return of Broadcast Liquor Ads," *All Politics: CNN Time*, November 9, 1996, <http://www.cnn.com/ALLPOLITICS/1996/news/9611/09/clinton.radio.address/index.shtml> (December 15, 2003).

13. American Medical Association, "NBC Does Right Thing," n.d., <http:// www.ama-assn.org/ama/pub/article/3216-6040.html> (November 7, 2002).

14. "Booze News: Expenditures for Alcoholic-beverage Advertising," *CSPI*, 2000, <http://www.cspinet.org/booze/liquor_branded_expenditures.htm> (November 7, 2002).

15. "Youth Got a Larger Glimpse of Alcohol from Advertisers Than Did Adults," *ChannelOne.com*, September 26, 2002, <http://www.channelonenews.com/articles/2002/09/26/ap_alcohol_ads/> (November 12, 2002).

16. Harris, p. 147.

17. Ibid., p. 149.

18. Ibid., p. 148.

19. Peterson, Nisenholz, and Robinson, p. 197.

20. "Alcohol and Tobacco on the Web: New Threats to Youth," *Center for Media Education*, March 1997, <http://www.cme.org/children/marketing/execsum.html> (November 7, 2002).

21. Peterson, Nisenholz, and Robinson, p. 202.

22. Harris, p. 157.

23. "Flawed Radio Advertising Study 'Blatantly Misleading,'" Distilled Spirits Council of the United States, press release, April 2, 2003, <http://www.discus.org/mediaroom/2003/release.asp?pressid=84> (June 6, 2003).

24. Harris, p. 133.

Chapter 7. Adolescents and Alcohol

1. Eric Newhouse, *Alcohol: Cradle to Grave* (Center City, Minn.: Hazelton Foundation, 2001), p. 200.

2. Nancy Bartley, "Alcohol Fatality Shows Dangers for Children," *The Seattle Times*, October 2, 2002, p. B2.

3. Michael Windle, *Alcohol Use Among Adolescents* (Thousand Oaks, Calif.: Sage Publications, 1999), p. 2.

4. "Alcohol and Teen Drinking," *Focus Adolescent Services*, 2001, <http://www.focusas.com/Alcohol. html> (September 12, 2002).

5. "Study: Underage Drinkers Starting at Earlier Age," *CNN.com:Health*, February 27, 2002, <http:// www.cnn.com/2002/HEALTH/parenting/02/26/teen. drinking> (October 7, 2002).

6. "Casa Study Reveals Dangerous Connection Between Teen Substance Use and Sex," National Center on Addiction and Substance Abuse at Columbia University, press release, December 7, 1999, <http://www. casacolumbia.org/absolutenm/templates/PressReleases. asp?articleid=136&zoneid=49> (December 23, 2003).

7. "Women and the Effects of Alcohol," *What You Need to Know About . . . Alcoholism*, n.d., <http:// alcoholism.about.com/library_weekly/aa000421a.htm> (November 18, 2002).

8. "Teen Drinking More Dangerous Than Previously Thought," *Monitor on Psychology*, vol. 32, no. 5, June 2001, <http://www.apa.org/monitor/jun01/teendrink. html> (April 13, 2002).

9. Peterson, Nisenholz, and Robinson, p. 66.

10. Ibid., p. 73.

11. Peter M. Monti, Suzanne M. Colby, and Tracy A. O'Leary, eds., *Adolescents, Alcohol, and Substance Abuse: Reaching Teens Through Brief Interventions* (New York: The Guilford Press, 2001), p. 201.

12. Patrick M. O'Malley, Lloyd D. Johnston, and Jerald G. Bachman, "Alcohol Use Among Adolescents," *NIAAA Web site*, 1998, <http://www.niaaa.nih.gov/publications/ arh22-2/85-94.pdf> (November 16, 2002).

13. Ibid.

14. Henry Wechsler et al., "College Alcohol Studies at Harvard, Trends in College Binge Drinking During a Period of Increased Prevention Efforts: Findings from 4 Harvard School of Public Health College Alcohol Study Surveys: 1993–2001," *Journal of American College Health*, vol. 50, no. 5, n.d., <http://www.hsphharvard.edu/cas/about/index.html> (November 16, 2002).

15. Susan Dentzer, "Binge Drinking," *KCTS Online: NewsHour*, April 10, 2002, <http://www.pbs.org/newshour/bb/health/jan-june02/drinking_4-10.html> (November 21, 2002).

16. Personal interview with Morgan Luce and Matthew Greenstreet, May 4, 2003.

17. Ibid.

18. Michael P. Haines, "A Social Norms Approach to Preventing Binge Drinking at Colleges and Universities," *Higher Education Center*, n.d., <http://www.edc.org/hec/pubs/socnorms.html> (June 1, 2003).

19. "University of Arizona: Alcohol Intervention," n.d., <http://www.socialnorm.org/arizinter.html> (June 1, 2003).

20. "National College Alcohol Study Finds No Evidence That Widely Used Alcohol Prevention Programs Reduce Student Drinking," *Harvard School of Public Health: College Alcohol Study*, July 24, 2003, <http://hsph.harvard.edu/cas/Documents/social_norms-press Release/>

21. Personal interview with student (name withheld), 2000.

22. Interview with Joanne Johnson, October 18, 2002.

23. Windle, p. 78.

24. Ibid., p. 86.

Chapter 8. Current Alcohol Issues

1. "A Major Contributor to the Nation's Economy," *Distilled Spirits Council of the United States*, 2001, <http://www.discus.org/about/background.htm> (December 2, 2002).

2. "Full Economic Impact of the Beer Industry to the

United States," *Beer Institute Online*, n.d., <http://www.beerinstitute.org/economicimpact.htm> (December 7, 2002).

3. Marcus Grant, "Letter from the President," *About ICAP, International Center for Alcohol Policies*, n.d., <http://www.icap.org/about_icap/about_icap.html> (November 13, 2002).

4. Eric Single, "Cost Estimates," *International Center for Alcohol Policies*, n.d., <http://www.icap.org/international/cost_estimates.html> (November 13, 2002).

5. Moira Plant, "Alcohol and Gender," *International Center for Alcohol Policies*, n.d., <http://www.icap.org/international/gender.html> (November 13, 2002).

6. "Treatment," *International Center for Alcohol Policies*, n.d., <http://www.icap.org/international/treatment.html> (November 13, 2002).

7. "Blood Alcohol Concentration Limits," *International Center for Alcohol Policies*, n.d., <http://www.icap.org/international/bac.html> (November 13, 2002).

8. "Harm Reduction and Alcohol Policies," *International Center for Alcohol Policies*, n.d., <http://www.icap.org/international/harm_reduction.html> (November 13, 2002).

9. "Advertising Self-Regulating," *International Center for Alcohol Policies*, n.d., <http://www.icap.org/international/self_regulation.html> (November 13, 2002).

10. "Binge Drinking," *International Center for Alcohol Policy: Policy Issues*, n.d., <http://www.icap.org/international/binge_drinking.html> (November 13, 2002).

11. "From Genes to Geography: the Cutting Edge of Alcohol Research," *NIAAA: Alcohol Alert*, July 2000, <http://www.niaaa.nih.gov/publications/aa48.htm> (October 31, 2002).

12. "Finally, A Pill for Alcoholism?" *What You Need to Know About . . . Alcoholism/Substance Abuse*, n.d., <http://alcoholism.about.com/cs/meds/a/aa030517.htm> (May 26, 2003).

Glossary

addiction—An obsessive behavior that cannot be broken without difficulty.

alcohol dependence (alcoholism)—An excessive need or craving for alcohol despite the fact that it causes physical and psychological problems.

Alcoholics Anonymous (AA)—A recovery program for people addicted to alcohol.

binge drinking—A period of heavy drinking often defined as five or more drinks in a row for men and four or more for women.

blood alcohol content or concentration (BAC) or blood alcohol level (BAL)—The ratio of alcohol to blood in the bloodstream. Expressed as a percentage.

comorbidity—The presence of more than one disorder in a person.

congeners—Substances combined with alcohol and water to produce the characteristic flavors, odors, and colors of particular alcoholic beverages.

distillation—A process of boiling alcohol with its fermented sugars and collecting the vapor to make pure alcohol.

DUI—Driving under the influence of alcohol.

fermentation—A natural process that occurs when yeast comes into contact with carbohydrates such as fruit, grains or honey and decomposes the sugars and converts them into CO_2 and alcohol.

fetal alcohol syndrome (FAS)—A pattern of birth

defects that sometimes appears in children whose mothers have abused alcohol when pregnant. A less severe syndrome is fetal alcohol effect, or FAE.

hangover—Nausea, headache, or other undesirable aftereffects following the drinking of alcohol.

intoxication—The state of being drunk or out of control after drinking alcohol.

liquor—an alcoholic beverage made by fermentation and distillation.

Mothers Against Drunk Driving (MADD)—An activist group that works for laws to combat drunk driving. Founded in 1980 as Mothers Against Drunk Drivers, the organization changed its name in 1984.

Prohibition—The period of time when alcohol was illegal in America.

proof—A measurement of the amount of pure alcohol in distilled spirits. The amount of alcohol is half the proof label; 100 proof contains 50 percent alcohol.

sobriety—The state of being sober, or not intoxicated.

Students Against Driving Drunk (SADD)—A activist organization for young people that fights drunk driving and promotes legal and safe alternatives to alcohol use. Founded in 1981, the group changed its name to Students Against Destructive Decisions in 1997 and expanded its mission to work against other unhealthy behaviors in addition to alcohol use.

temperance movement—An organized attempt to get drinkers to moderate or stop their use of alcohol.

tolerance—A state where a drinker needs increasing amounts of alcohol to experience its desired effects.

withdrawal—Negative physical and psychological responses experienced when alcohol is taken away from a drinker who is dependent upon alcohol.

For More Information

Mothers Against Drunk Driving (MADD)
511 E. John Carpenter Freeway, Suite 700
Irving, Tex. 75062
Phone: 1-800-GET-MADD
Fax: 1-972-869-2206/7

Students Against Destructive Decisions (SADD)
P.O. Box 800
Marlboro, Mass. 01752
Phone: 1-877-SADD-INC
Fax: 1-508-481-5759

Alcoholics Anonymous (AA)
Mailing Address:
Grand Central Station
P.O. Box 459
New York, N.Y. 10163

Al-Anon and Alateen
1600 Corporate Landing Parkway
Virginia Beach, Va. 23454-5617
Phone: 1-757-563-1600
Fax: 1-757-563-1655

National Association for Children of Alcoholics (NACoA)
11426 Rockville Pike, Suite 100
Rockville, Md. 20852
Phone: 1-888-55-4COAS
Fax: 1-301-468-0987

Further Reading

Books

Carson-DeWitt, Rosalyn. *Drugs, Alcohol, and Tobacco: Learning about Addictive Behavior.* Farmington Hills, Mich.: Gale Group, 2002.

Graves, Bonnie. *Alcohol Use and Abuse.* Mankato, Minn.: LifeMatters, 2000.

Hyde, Margaret O., and John F. Setaro. *Alcohol 101: An Overview for Teens.* Brookfield, Conn.: Twenty-First Century Books, 1999.

Johnson, Julie. *Why Do People Drink Alcohol?* Austin, Texas: Raintree Steck-Vaughn, 2001.

Landau, Elaine. *Alcohol.* New York: Scholastic Library Publishing, 2003.

Miller, Andrew. *Alcohol and Your Liver: The Incredibly Disgusting Story.* New York: The Rosen Group, Inc., 2000.

Internet Addresses

Neuroscience for Kids: Alcohol
<http://faculty.washington.edu/chudler/alco.html>

The Cool Spot
<http://www.thecoolspot.gov>

National Association for Children of Alcoholics Just 4 Kids
<http://www.nacoa.net/kidspage.htm>

Index